STEPS IN TIME

STEPS IN TIME

Ninety Years of
Metro Parks, Serving Summit County

Your Back Yard for 90 Years

Sarah Vradenburg

RINGTAW BOOKS
AKRON, OHIO

Robert Bogdanski 2011

15   14   13   12   11   5   4   3   2   1

ISBN 978-1-935603-66-5 (paperback)
LCCN 2011934853

The paper used in this publication meets the minimum requirements of American National Standard for Information Sciences—Permanence of Paper for Printed Library Materials, ANSI Z39.48–1984. ∞

Editor, Project Manager: Nathan Eppink, Chief of Marketing & Communications, Metro Parks, Serving Summit County
Art Director: Karl Simonson, Graphic Designer / Production Coordinator, Metro Parks, Serving Summit County

Contents

Acknowledgments   vii

Introduction   ix

1   The First Steps   1

2   The Treasure Hunt Begins   9

3   Making Places for People   29

4   Getting People into the Parks   50

5   Going Natural   62

6   Peace in the Valley   84

7   Long and Winding Trails   98

8   Making Friends   111

9   The Gorge   122

10   Further Steps   132

Appendix   137

Sources   143

In 1785, tribal leaders from the Chippewa, Delaware, Ottawa and Wyandot met with representatives sent by Congress to sign the Treaty of Fort McIntosh (*above*). The treaty surrendered control of Native American lands in southern and eastern Ohio to the U.S. government. Today, Treaty Line Road in Sand Run Metro Park delineates the eastern section of the treaty-imposed Native American territory—and the western boundary of the United States. The Portage Path, the trail used by Native Americans to portage between the Cuyahoga and Tuscarawas rivers, also became a part of this boundary line.

Acknowledgments

If history is the thread that connects one age to another, I owe my first thanks to the Boston Township trustees who, in 1921, took some good advice and asked the courts to create a metropolitan park in Summit County. Had it not been for them, none of the rest of this would have been possible.

In that vein, I also want to give credit to pioneering director-secretary Harold S. Wagner, whose imprint continues to be felt throughout this park system and parks throughout the country. From the system's farsighted plans, to its meticulous maintenance, to its bedrock mission of preserving this county's blessings of open space, I could see the origins in Wagner's letters and feisty, single-minded attitude. I also have special gratitude for pioneering naturalist Bert Szabo. In 1991, Szabo left full-time employment with the park district to volunteer nearly full-time sorting and organizing Wagner's voluminous correspondence. His devotion and attention to detail made my job as a researcher infinitely easier. And his example of service lights a path forward for us all.

I couldn't have asked for better help than I received from the brainy and conscientious folks who tend the Special Collections Department at the Akron-Summit County Public Library, led ably and affably by Judy

James. They safeguard Akron's historic heartbeat; they know it and do it with great pride. And the librarians at the *Akron Beacon Journal* were always eager to share their piece of this historic jigsaw puzzle.

So, too, do I appreciate the many hours Metro Parks Naturalist Mike Greene spent showing me each of the parks, pointing out nooks and crannies that word folk like me might miss. Greene, and his colleagues in Interpretive Services, also offered valuable guidance in shaping the manuscript. This is not to slight any of the other Metro Parks staff, from division chiefs down, who have been very tolerant of my comings and goings, making sure I had access to whatever material I might need. And I must acknowledge the earlier park history, *75 Years of Treasures and Pleasures* by the late Patricia Zonsius. Her work is the foundation on which *Steps in Time* is built.

Of course, I thank current director-secretary Keith Shy for being approachable, open and who let this book unfold as it did. Thanks also to the Board of Park Commissioners of Metro Parks, Serving Summit County, for giving me this opportunity. Although Rainy Stitzlein is no longer a commissioner, her personal encouragement at crucial moments gave me a needed boost. I count Frances Seiberling Buchholzer as a personal friend; she honors her family legacy with her service. And Carol Curtis' stories of her personal connection to these parks only underscored something my research made clear to me: People love these parks and will work tirelessly on their behalf. I also want to thank former chief of communications, Susan Fairweather, and her successor, Nathan Eppink, for offering me this unique opportunity and for shepherding it through to completion.

This book isn't so much the history of a physical entity as it is a history of the relationship between the public and their parks. As with any relationship, things have not always gone smoothly or easily. The key has been tenacity and, at least at the outset, faith in the new concept of public parks. It is impossible to imagine Summit County without its magnificent green islands, yet things could have turned out very differently. What tipped the scale was the spirit of service that Wagner inculcated, which lives on in today's park staff and officials, and the people's unmistakable affection for their parks. It is an enduring and unbeatable combination.

Sarah Vradenburg

Introduction

History is made every day in the Metro Parks. People meet. Children learn. Families reunite. It's the natural setting of the Metro Parks that attracts them.

Since the beginning, the Akron Metropolitan Park District—now Metro Parks, Serving Summit County—has preserved wild places for exploration and conservation. Harold S. Wagner, the park district's first director-secretary, stressed the importance of natural-area parks. In that respect, though much has transpired, little has changed in ninety years.

Visitors, volunteers and park employees share in the legacy of early visionaries like Wagner, the Olmsted Brothers—whose land-acquisition plan set the course for decades—and F.A. Seiberling, an early park commissioner who helped jump-start the formation of Sand Run and some of today's most visited Metro Parks. As stewards of the park district's natural resources, we all continue to write its history.

Nathan Eppink, Chief of Marketing & Communications
Metro Parks, Serving Summit County

CHAPTER ONE

The First Steps

I T TAKES A BROAD BRUSH to paint a picture of Summit County's park district. It's not just a portrait of land or people, animals or wildlife. It's all of that, and more. It is a story of vision, timing and the coming together of people and movements that created something priceless that continues to grow in value.

By the turn of the twentieth century, the nation was beginning to realize the importance of saving natural resources. There already were several national parks and monuments, thanks largely to visionaries such as John Muir and Teddy Roosevelt. Congress created the National Park Service in 1916 to hold lands that were coming into federal control. Still, there were few protections for local preserves. As cities grew and industrialization shifted people from the countryside to urban areas, state and local natural resources faced a serious threat.

Cleveland Metroparks commissioners and park planners review drawings for their Brecksville Reservation in 1920. *Courtesy of Cleveland Metroparks*

William A. Stinchcomb, Cleveland's self-taught surveyor and engineer, saw this clearly. He hounded Cleveland officials and the Ohio General Assembly tirelessly to save regional open space, even though most of the space he sought to save was not within city limits. He said, as early as 1905, if something was not done, housing and industry would eventually devour priceless natural treasures.

In 1911, state lawmakers eventually gave counties the power to create metropolitan park districts that were neither city, state nor federal. They did not, however, give those districts any power other than the ability to accept donations of land and cash and to manage what they were given. These districts had no taxing authority, and as creatures of county commissioners they were vulnerable to political whims. Still, that legal go-ahead spurred Cleveland—always led by Stinchcomb—to hire Frederick Law Olmsted, the architect of New York's famous Central Park. Olmsted drew up a map of lands in Cleveland and Cuyahoga County worthy of preservation. All was set to go forward until a lawsuit challenged the limited authority of the park districts. The courts ruled that because park commissioners were not elected officials, they had no right to spend public money.

Stinchcomb flew into action, prodding the legislature—even drafting the bill—to make needed changes. In March 1917, the Ohio Legislature gave oversight of the districts to a county's elected probate judge, who then would appoint three park commissioners, satisfying one of the court's objections. Even more important, the new law gave districts taxing authority. Within three months, Cuyahoga County had a park system. Summit County followed four years later.

The year 1917 was also when Harold S. Wagner, then twenty-four, stepped off the train from Boston at Union Station. Trained at Harvard's Arnold Arboretum, the slight landscape architect had been brought to Akron by Warren Manning. Manning, long an associate of Central Park's Frederick Law Olmsted, had discovered Wagner laboring gratis

F. A. Seiberling at his
desk. *Courtesy of Stan Hywet
Hall and Gardens*

F.A. Seiberling's estate, Stan Hywet.
Courtesy of Stan Hywet Hall and Gardens

for Olmsted's firm. Seeing his talent, Manning put Wagner on his own payroll. He had a specific client in Akron in mind for Wagner's horticultural knowledge and attention to detail.

Manning was knee-deep in landscape design and construction for F.A. Seiberling's newly-built country estate, Stan Hywet. Actually, Manning had other Seiberling projects in mind for Wagner. Goodyear's founder, Seiberling, had just proved his critics wrong with the success of the workingman's neighborhood, Goodyear Heights, which he created up the hill from his East Market Street tire factory. After the grounds of his own home were complete, Seiberling turned his sights to building an upscale version of Goodyear Heights for the well-heeled residents of the area, many of whom were his junior executives at Goodyear. He gave the job to Manning, who in turn gave the job to the able Wagner, who was already busy building another of Manning's many Akron-area landmarks, the Fairlawn Golf Club.

Wagner set to work in the wooded knolls near the golf course, an ideal natural setting for Fairlawn Heights, Akron's exclusive neighborhood of rambling, elegant homes and curving, tree-shaded streets.

Once those jobs were complete, Seiberling was loath to let Wagner return east. He persuaded Akron officials to hire him as superintendent of the city's parks. As such, Wagner was at the table during talks about how to take advantage of the new state law that allowed the formation of countywide park districts.

The first step to create a district required a petition from a governmental unit to the county's probate judge. Boston Township—with Cleve-

Harold S. Wagner, first director-secretary of the Akron Metropolitan Park District

land's Stinchcomb pointing the way—made such a petition to Summit County Common Pleas Probate Judge Lewis Slusser in 1921.

There was more to Boston Township's request than pure civic altruism. Trustees were fed up with Akron polluting the Cuyahoga River, which flowed through the township's heart at Peninsula. Akron, the township's upstream neighbor, had nearly tripled its population between 1910 and 1920, and its small sewage treatment plant on Cuyahoga Street was no match for its nearly 210,000 residents and burgeoning industry. After several official complaints from the trustees to the state health department, the township agreed to petition for a Summit County park district, thinking, wishfully it turned out, that a countywide conservation movement focusing on the vast and storied Cuyahoga Valley might force Akron to clean up after itself. The trustees' petition was granted December

31, 1921, and the Akron Metropolitan Park District was formed, but only after Hudson and Twinsburg Township opted out.

(Akron would open a new sewage treatment plant in 1928 at Botzum. Sadly, the city's hasty building boom commingled storm runoff and sanitary sewage, a problem that plagues the Cuyahoga River to this day.)

When the park district was created, the county did not suddenly sprout forest preserves overnight. It took nearly three years before Judge Slusser appointed commissioners. In 1923, James Shaw of Colonial Salt, community leader, educator and environmentalist Maude Milar and Charles Raymond of B.F. Goodrich, were named the district's first commissioners. But even that was not enough to get things moving. Most of the first two years were spent creating studies of recreational opportunities at Springfield Lake and whether it was feasible to build a parkway between Akron and Medina. With the area growing fast, the commissioners did not seem to think that the first order of business ought to be preserving land.

By 1925, with the park district spinning its wheels, Slusser shook up the board, replacing two of three commissioners. He replaced Shaw and Raymond with F.A. Seiberling, who by this time had created and was running Seiberling Rubber, and Edmund Eckroad of the Northern Ohio Traction and Light Company—forerunner of today's FirstEnergy. Seiberling again turned to Wagner, still in charge of Akron's city parks. Wagner, in turn, suggested the board hire the Olmsted Brothers—sons of Frederick Law Olmsted—to survey the area. He went as far as to guide his former colleagues throughout Summit County. Their report was complete in three months.

It is no surprise that the beautiful Cuyahoga Valley headed the Olmsteds' list. They were impressed with its expanse and, for industrial Northeast Ohio, its relatively unspoiled condition (while noting the "present obnoxious and dangerous condition of the river"). While the Olmsted Brothers strongly advocated a system of scenic easements to preserve

Dressed in their finest, this group poses for a portrait in 1910 by the Cuyahoga Falls on the Cuyahoga River. Today, the falls are under water.

the landscape and scenery, they advised against making the entire area into a park. Such a park would be larger than the population of Summit County would ever need, they believed. More, they said it would be too hard to police and maintain, and would take too much productive land off the tax duplicate.

Second on the list, after the Cuyahoga Valley, came the Cuyahoga River Gorge in Cuyahoga Falls, dammed in 1910 by the Northern Ohio Traction and Light to generate hydroelectricity for its streetcars. Among other places the Olmsteds believed warranted preservation were ravines surrounding Mud Brook, on the eastern slope of the Cuyahoga Valley; Sand Run, the Yellow Creek Valley, Boston Run, Brandywine Creek and Furnace Run. They placed great emphasis on overlooks, and made note of the Wintergreen Ledges, in what is now the Rolling Acres area, the Ritchie Ledges (later part of Virginia Kendall State Park), the Twinsburg Ledges (now part of Liberty Park), Turkeyfoot Reservation (excluding the remainder of the Portage Lakes), Springfield Lake and the canal and lake system between Akron and Barberton. They also suggested using the Cuyahoga River north of the Gorge for boating and canoeing, and Lake Rockwell and the Barberton Reservoir for recreation.

A final and less successful element of their report was devoted to advocating for a significant network of parkways throughout the county. Even at that time, the Olmsteds understood the value of the remaining canal lands and urged the construction of a parkway along the canal route from the Tuscarawas Valley south of Barberton—with perhaps the creation of an elongated park along the canal lands—north to the Little Cuyahoga and Cuyahoga rivers, connecting with Sand Run and Yellow Creek. Their ultimate goal was to connect with the growing Cleveland Metroparks system through Hinckley and the Rocky River Valley and Furnace Run, north to Brecksville Reservation, the Cuyahoga River Valley at Brandywine to Tinkers Creek and north to the Chagrin River Reservation.

A year later, Seiberling persuaded his fellow commissioners to hire Wagner away from the city parks to direct the fledgling, floundering park district. The native Bostonian accepted the position of director-secretary, using the Olmsted report as his guiding light for the next thirty-two years.

CHAPTER TWO

The Treasure Hunt Begins

JUST BECAUSE THE Olmsteds didn't think it wise to preserve the entire Cuyahoga Valley didn't mean there weren't vast stretches of land that needed to be saved, and quickly. Akron and Cleveland were growing. The opportunity might slip away.

Park commissioners had already looked at the Gorge longingly, particularly after the Olmsted report placed it so high on its list of priorities. Residents of Akron and Cuyahoga Falls were familiar with it, not for its scenic beauty, but as the home to Riverview Amusement Park and Old Maid's Kitchen, or Mary Campbell Cave. The Gorge would have to wait.

With Sand Run figuring prominently in the Olmsted report, F.A. Seiberling took the lead, offering a massive chunk of his estate as the district's first major acquisition.

Seiberling's lifelong passion for healthful living had spurred him to move his family from their home on East Market Street to a hilltop overlooking

9

the Cuyahoga Valley. Their city address was more convenient to his work, but it was downwind of the soot and grime spewed by the city's iconic rubber companies. His move heralded a population shift in Akron to the west.

Within the more than three thousand acres Seiberling amassed for his country estate was Sand Run, a Cuyahoga River tributary cloaked in virgin forests. It was through its lush ravines and along the creek's meandering path that Wagner, in his role as Warren Manning's boots on the ground, had already built the bridle paths used by Seiberling's many famous guests.

The park board already had a nugget of a park nearby in tiny, .176-acre Courtney Park, donated in 1925 as part of Akron's centennial. It was not so much a donation to the park board as it was an acknowledgement of the importance of the Portage Path in ancient history.

Joseph Courtney's dairy farm hugged the west side of that Indian pathway, and he wanted people to remember the area's importance. He donated a tiny chunk of land which was all but useless to him. The Daughters of the American Revolution commissioned a bronze plaque which was attached to a boulder in the park in honor of Akron's 100th birthday. The Courtney Park boulder and plaque—or its replacement after the original plaque was stolen—remain at the southwest corner of the intersection of North Portage Path and Merriman Road. Subsequent road improvements have placed the park much closer to the Portage Path than its original location.

Courtney's opening move put Seiberling on the spot. Despite leasing some of his land at no cost to the park board for a tree nursery, the neighborhood's largest landholder had been upstaged.

"It was then F.A. Seiberling, a little irked by the irony of the park board possessing less than an acre of land, donated the first strip of what is now Sand Run (Metro Park)" said *Akron Beacon Journal* reporter Mabel Norris, in a brief 1936 history of the park district.

Seiberling's first donation was nearly five hundred acres, stretching from Merriman Road to what is now Ghent Road near Summit Mall,

Courtney Park was marked with a plaque and boulder, which now sits near the intersection of Portage Path and Merriman Road.

following the stream and bridle path and encompassing what had been the Portage Game Preserve. Using that as leverage, Wagner and his colleagues on the board approached the remaining thirty-one local landowners, either to donate rights of way along the future Sand Run Parkway or to sell their land outright. By the time the parkway opened to the public in April 1929, it comprised close to seven hundred acres, with a perimeter of about twelve miles.

Setting this area aside as a park accomplished two major goals: It preserved a magnificent landscape rich in its potential for hiking, education and family recreation. It also saved this area's link to the nation's history, both through the Portage Path and to the War of 1812.

Still, Wagner's mission was far larger than saving one piece of property, no matter how large, beautiful or historical. The time was ripe to make good on the Olmsteds' vision. There were a lot of people or companies with land on the Olmsted wish list. At the same time Wagner was gathering land for Sand Run, he and Seiberling were wooing the son of Cleveland inventor and industrialist Charles F. Brush for several hundred acres at the headwaters of another Cuyahoga tributary, Furnace Run.

Brush Sr. had invented the electric arc light, making Cleveland the first city in the nation to have electric streetlights. He purchased the 2,100-acre Richfield farm of Everett Farnham, one of the township's first settlers and an avid conservationist. The Brush family regularly spent their summers and holidays there, sharing it generously with Richfield residents, continuing Farnham's tradition of opening his farm to his Richfield neighbors for hiking and recreation.

Seiberling knew about the land because several years earlier he had tried to buy some of it from the elder Brush. Had he succeeded, Stan Hywet might now be in Richfield Township or bulldozed by the Ohio Turnpike and Interstate 77. Luckily for Summit County, Brush turned him down.

Although Brush Sr. was still alive, he had given the farm to his son and namesake by 1927. Still, Wagner and Seiberling called on the elder Brush first. Seiberling reminded the Cleveland inventor of their previous meeting. "We have met before," he told Brush Sr. "At that time I tried to buy this land from you for myself. Now, sir, I am asking you to give it to the county."

Eventually, Seiberling's powers of persuasion convinced Brush Jr. that a donation of 450 acres, including the virgin beech forest, would be a boon to the county and a feather in his cap. However, in May 1927, just two weeks after reaching an agreement in principle with the park board, Charles Brush Jr. died during a blood transfusion, in a vain attempt to save his daughter Jane, who was dying of pneumonia.

His wife, Dorothy Hamilton Brush, grieving the near-simultaneous loss of husband and child, did not immediately follow through with her late husband's donation. Thankfully, she also didn't follow her father-in-law's $50,000 monetary lead and offer some of her land as a camp

Dorothy Hamilton Brush posted this sign on her property, inviting the public to use it as a park.

for children with tuberculosis. Instead, she performed a unique social experiment, testing the public's readiness for a park. Against family and legal advice, she threw open her farm to everyone, not just Richfield residents, with this invitation on a signpost near the entrance: *Dear Public: They say if I let you picnic here you will ruin my property. I don't believe it, so will try my experiment for a year. Please back me up by building no fires and disposing of all your rubbish. If you pick the wild flowers there will not be any another year. This is a game preserve, so do not shoot. Mrs. Charles F. Brush Jr., Brush Farm*

A year later, she had proved the naysayers wrong and extended the pubic invitation for another year. She also eventually offered some of her land as a camp for ailing children, naming it the Jane Brush Camp. In the meantime, she decided her husband's original impulse was sound, and quietly donated 275 acres to the Akron Metropolitan Park District. The deed was finalized in 1929.

The property was long and skinny, running north and south along Furnace Run, the beginning of what the park board envisioned as a

Cleveland children play on the Brush property in Furnace Run, 1932

parkway linking the Cuyahoga Valley to the Cleveland Metroparks system, either in Brecksville or Hinckley, as suggested by the Olmsteds. At some points the park was six hundred feet wide, sometimes two thousand feet wide. It encompassed the Furnace Run headwaters and the beech woods across from what was then sleepy U.S. Route 21. It also included the area of Furnace Run in the Cuyahoga Valley, crossed by the Everett Road covered bridge, which the park board turned into its main tree nursery.

As a condition of the sale, Mrs. Brush asked that a boulder be placed near the park entrance that paid tribute to her late husband. A granite boulder was found soon enough, inscribed and installed. Later, the placement put it directly in the path of improvements to U.S. Route 21. The boulder eventually found a permanent home in the park on Old Mill Trail. Hikers who pass it can still read the inscription, which comes from *God of the Open Air* by Henry Van Dyke, one of Brush Jr.'s favorite poets.

Even as they were finalizing details with Mrs. Brush, board members were pursuing other property. In 1929, the board took reluctant nearby

The Brushwood memorial boulder, shown at its unveiling, is visible today along Old Mill Trail.

property owners Townsend and Rice to court in its first test of eminent domain powers. It would be years, but eventually the forty-two acres controlled by the Townsend family would become part of the park.

By 1929, there was much bustle in the park board's office on the second floor of the Summit County Courthouse. In addition to building Sand Run Parkway, accepting several parcels near Springfield Lake from the family of Minnie Acker (eventually returned to her heirs) and finalizing the deed for the core of the Furnace Run Reservation, the board and Wagner were also finally negotiating to acquire the Cuyahoga River Gorge in Cuyahoga Falls.

Its wild beauty—most spectacularly its 105-foot waterfall and many caves—made it a popular tourist attraction, even before the Civil War. Later, the High Bridge Glens resort, built in 1878 by L.W. Loomis and Harvey Parks, not only had a very popular two-story dance hall, but also what its owners boasted as the nation's first roller coaster. With a popular amusement park alongside the magnificent falls, boat companies sold trips from the city's downtown to the falls and back for a dime.

It remained a tourist attraction and home to the Riverview Amusement Park, even after Kent and Cuyahoga Falls began dumping raw sewage up river early in the twentieth century. However, the crowds thinned in 1910 after Northern Ohio Traction and Light dammed the river to produce hydroelectricity.

By 1929, Riverview had defaulted on its lease. NOTL officials were negotiating a new lease, this time with shareholders of the Fairyland Amusement Park. The new company—owned by many of Riverview's former shareholders—had promised to take over Riverview's assets and clean the place up, as long as they could continue to use it as an amusement park. Fortunately, the lease was never executed. Prompted by then-park board member and NOTL executive Edmund Eckroad, the electricity company gave the park district the deed to the Gorge, a welcome Christmas present in December 1929 and a morale boost to area residents in the months following the stock market crash. What made the gift even more meaningful, and would prove important decades later, was that it abutted Akron's High Bridge Park, a popular turn-of-the-century picnic and playground.

Wagner has been described, by fans and critics alike, as a purist, far more eager to preserve nature than to provide places for people to play. While those characterizations are accurate, he also never turned down a chance to make the park district a little money. So it was that the park board went into the dance-hall rental business.

It is clear from reading park correspondence that Fairyland Amusement's owners didn't really want the roller coaster or other popular money-losers. Fairyland's principals really only wanted the profitable pieces: the ballroom and, after Cuyahoga Falls outlawed Sunday dancing, the refreshment stands. They had hoped that, because the park district was its own unit of government, park rules would supersede local anti-dancing laws. Park correspondence suggests Wagner gave serious thought to pressing the issue.

The Roseland Ballroom, shown in fall 1930, stood on what is now Gorge Metro Park.

Construction of Gorge Shelter by CCC workers, February 1937

In 1933, workers cleaned up the land donated by Goodyear Tire & Rubber to help form Goodyear Heights Metropolitan Park.

As timing would have it, Akron decided to permit Sunday dancing, and the Falls followed suit rather than miss out on potential income. The Gorge, sitting as it does between the two cities, was in a position to cater to customers from both communities. It looked like a great deal—the income would help keep the Gorge self-supporting. Although voters had approved the board's first levy request in 1928, the Depression ensured that property tax collections would not equal pre-crash estimates, and every spare dime was earmarked for acquisition.

The board leased the dance hall and toilets to Fairyland Amusements for $500 a season. Fairyland got the better deal. Park records show the company made about $2,000 a month, while causing headaches for the district, including parking problems, fights and maintenance hassles. Despite the income, the dance hall operators rarely paid on time and eventually stopped paying altogether.

The dance hall would go on to have other owners and its name would change from the Fairyland Dance Hall to the Roseland Ballroom, but the dance hall itself remained until 1936. Once the district was ready to build a new park shelter, it disassembled the old dance hall and moved it to Elizabeth Park, where it was reconstructed as a recreation shelter. It has since been razed, some of the stone remaining in the landscape at the Cascade Village housing development.

By 1930, the park district was nearing one thousand acres, none of it actually inside the city of Akron. While that proved the wisdom of the metropolitan park concept, it left Akron residents with inadequate parks, while still paying taxes to the new district. With the Great Depression settling in, there was a sense among board members that people needed open space and recreation closer to their homes. A former Akron resident made 1930 the right time to consider the first metropolitan park inside the city.

Real estate broker Gilbert Waltz had contacted the board in 1929 about donating land he owned in East Akron. His wife, Jessie, had died in 1925, and he wanted to offer something in her memory. He also said he felt obliged to give something back to the community that had given him so much. Waltz, a onetime Akron grocer and farmer, had moved to Los Angeles ten years earlier, but remained fond of the city and returned each year to check on property he still owned.

As Waltz told his story, he owed much of his prosperity to Seiberling, having helped the rubber magnate acquire the land for Goodyear Heights, while keeping some for himself. In 1930, Waltz offered the board 37.53 acres he owned west of Darrow Road and north of Newton Street. At the same time, Seiberling's real estate firm, Goodyear Heights Realty, was preparing to donate 34.5 acres in the same area if the county would forgive its sewer assessments. The nugget for Goodyear Heights Metro Park was in hand. However, this new park was far from pristine.

"I remember after Goodyear gave it to us, we went out there and spent about three weeks with a truck and four or five men hauling away all the tin cans and rubbish that was piled up," Wagner recalled in 1971.

The Depression's devastation would help the board acquire more city land for the Goodyear Heights Metropolitan Park than it could otherwise have afforded. Another firm, Eastland Development, fell behind on its mortgage to First City Trust. The firm secured $18,000 in property tax abatements on fifty-three acres, as long as the land was donated to the park board, enlarging the original seventy-two acres to 125 by the middle of 1930.

Bad economies make for historic irony. The park board bought a beautiful piece of land at the corner of Darrow Road and Newton Street owned by local physicians Miller and McKay that Wagner had once designed as a subdivision. The doctors' plans derailed in the market crash, and after the state took over the banks it put the Miller-McKay land up for sale. Tallmadge Township paid $8,000 for a ten-acre parcel for a school, and the park board bought the remaining 120 acres for $4,000.

This park, a patchwork quilt stitched together from tiny lots either donated or purchased with a later grant of $30,000 from Goodyear Tire & Rubber, was slow to flesh out. With the exception of a 115-acre donation in 1941 by First Central Trust, forerunner of First National Bank, it would take the park board until 1963 to acquire all of the park's current 410 acres. In 1966, a swap of land at Goodyear Heights between the city of Akron and the park board bolstered negotiations with donors and helped create Hampton Hills Metro Park. (At that time, the city needed a high point on the east side of town for a water tower. The perfect place existed at Goodyear Heights. At the same time, the park board was talking with Reginald and Rhea Adam about donating their Top O' the World acreage and needed frontage on Akron-Peninsula Road that the city owned and had once used for a workhouse garden.)

As the Akron Metropolitan Park District grew in size—in 1932 it controlled more than 1,600 acres—it was also growing in reputation, which came in handy as the fate of Virginia Kendall State Park was decided.

Two couples and a dog pose for a photograph at Ice Box Cave in the Kendall Ledges, August 1939

Hayward Kendall, who made his fortune first in coal and then oil, had purchased nearly four hundred acres, known widely as the Ritchie Ledges, in Boston Township. It was one of the prime overlook spots mentioned in the Olmsted report. Kendall's property was adjacent to Camp Manatoc, owned by the then-Akron Council of the Boy Scouts, and Camp Ledgewood, owned by the Girl Scouts, making it prime wilderness. Kendall used the area as a private retreat and hunting lodge. When the oil tycoon died in 1928 of complications of pneumonia, his will set the stage for a potential land grab.

At one point before his death, Kendall had offered a $1 million endowment to Cornell University if its trustees would close the school to women and shutter the fraternities. They refused and Kendall took his millions elsewhere.

He left his entire estate to his wife except for the land, which she had never liked. Kendall's will was clear on only one point: The ledges were to remain a public park. As for heirs, the will created several possibilities; the first to say yes got the land, along with a trust fund to underwrite the park's operations. Kendall insisted the park be named for his mother, Virginia Hutchinson Kendall.

Kendall's first choice was the federal government, which turned it down as land unsuitable for a national park. Next on the list was the State of Ohio. If Ohio turned it down, the park board of the city of Cleveland were to be offered the land. If no one would take it on, Kendall's will stipulated that trustees appointed by Central National Bank operate it as a public park. Wagner recalled visiting Kendall in New York to talk to him about the potential donation of the Ledges to the park district, but a quirk of scheduling kept the men from meeting before Kendall died. It may be that lost opportunity that kept the Akron Metropolitan Park District from being listed as a potential heir.

The state accepted the land in 1929. However, Wagner was concerned because he felt Ohio's parks were not very well managed. He and Seiberling persuaded the state legislature to put it under the control of Edmund Secrest, state forester, who reported to Ohio State University. Wagner and Secrest knew each other well. At first Wagner was confident the land would be well cared for.

"But Secrest sent some flunkies up here and they began to cut all the merchantable timber on the place. We raised Cain because people thought it was our property and they began to blame us," Wagner said.

To avert an arboreal disaster, he and Seiberling began to lobby the state legislature to have the Akron district manage the area as a park and not a logging operation. By that time the park district had made a good name for itself, and because Seiberling still wielded enormous political clout, the Ohio Legislature and OSU trustees made that change on September

29, 1933. Eventually, Virginia Kendall State Park would encompass 1,600 acres, effectively doubling the district's holdings.

While this drama was played out on one set of sandstone ledges, another quietly unfolded at a stone outcropping in nearby Peninsula, with the help of a *Cleveland Plain Dealer* humorist. The Olmsted report reflected on the region's rich sandstone deposits, and no area was better known than this part of the Cuyahoga Valley, where sandstone had been quarried for more than a century. Richard Howe, who oversaw the construction of the Ohio & Erie Canal, quarried some of the stone for the project from an outcropping on the west side of the Cuyahoga River, south of Peninsula. Akron's Ferdinand Schumacher, whose rolled oats made Akron and Quaker Oats a household name, also quarried his millstones from property he owned for a short time in this area.

The Cleveland Quarries, which purchased the quarries in the late nineteenth century, stopped active quarrying by 1917. In 1931, *Plain Dealer* columnist Fred Kelly, who owned six hundred acres on the other side of the river, had gotten wind that the company wanted to donate it for parkland. He sought out Seiberling with the news, telling him that company officials had approached Cleveland Metroparks first. However, when Seiberling met with company officials, he made a very persuasive case that the land should go to the Akron Metropolitan Park District, because it was in Summit County.

Kelly, in correspondence with Wagner, gave another compelling rationale: "This gift will mark the first important donation of land along this main route between the two cities and may be an opening wedge by which many other land owners may be shamed into giving land free or at low cost." Kelly saw the need for a Cuyahoga Valley park four decades before one would be created.

Company officials found this argument persuasive, but took their time in deciding. By 1934, the Akron Metropolitan Park District owned or

Quarrymen pose on the quarry steps in Peninsula, pre-1917

was developing Sand Run, Furnace Run, the Gorge, Goodyear Heights and Virginia Kendall. When Cleveland Quarry officials told Kelly they would give the quarry to the district on the condition that park officials convinced them they had a plan, Wagner swung into action. He showed them what the district had accomplished in less than a decade. Moreover, by 1934, the federal government had created the Civilian Conservation Corps, and Wagner already had plans for the parks and for the stone the district might acquire. Indeed, he had already approached the quarry owners for stone for the other parks' CCC-built shelters.

The quarry steps, shown here in the 1930s, now rise like ancient ruins in the woods of Deep Lock Quarry Metro Park.

The strategy worked. In February 1934, the Cleveland Quarries deeded their land to the Akron Metropolitan Park District, while reserving the right to sell sandstone for an unspecified period of time. Even though the company no longer actively cut stone, the Depression made them rethink their options. As Cleveland Quarries chairman wrote Wagner in July 1934, the company sold about $350 worth of stone that year, "and $350 looks like a lot of money to us these days." Later that same year, the state leased land north of the Cleveland Quarries holdings, that had once been owned by Capt. Howe, to the district. Today, the seventy-three-acre Deep Lock Quarry Metro Park takes its name from Lock 28, which was the deepest of the locks between Akron and Cleveland along the Ohio & Erie Canal.

It would be nearly another decade before Cleveland Quarries stopped quarrying sandstone, but the parks and the region got the better of this deal. In 1937, Wagner wrote company officials about five park structures that had been built, at least in part, by CCC crews using stone from the Peninsula quarry. The open-air theater in Akron's Chestnut Ridge city park, a Works Progress Administration project, also was built using park sandstone, as was the building for Akron's Italian Unione Abruzzese. Many of the park roads built during the 1930s, including the completion of Sand Run Parkway and roads into Virginia Kendall State Park, had Peninsula sandstone beds.

In 1936, the park board began leasing property abutting the Sand Run holdings, between Merriman Road and Portage Path, that Summit County had once purchased for a hospital. While the hospital never materialized, the park board's success with the CCC made its proposal to build an amphitheater at the top of Portage Path hill using the Works Progress Administration, very attractive. As early as 1938, as the park board began to outgrow its offices in the county courthouse, it began to look at this site for permanent offices.

A look at a mid-1930s park map would show that all of the park property was either in central or northern Summit County. The southern end was beginning to develop and there was growing pressure to find land for a park south of Akron. At the same time, Firestone Tire & Rubber was eager to become well-known park donors like Goodyear's Seiberling.

Ever on the prowl for good parkland, Wagner found nothing large enough in the southern part of the county that was worth calling a park. With the Depression dragging on, there was precious little money to buy large tracts. So, in the late 1930s, when Firestone's real estate agent James Groark visited Wagner with a proposal from Firestone, the park director was eager to listen.

Firestone was willing to donate land near the old feeder canal, almost directly opposite of the then-clubhouse of the Firestone golf course. Wagner was not impressed. After looking at the land, he advised the commissioners against accepting it because, "It was neither a metropolitan

The Tuscarawas Race, passing through Firestone Metropolitan Park in 1941.

park or anything of which the Firestone Tire & Rubber Co. would ever be proud."

Groark took the news back to Firestone's executives. A few months passed and the real estate man returned, this time suggesting a much better arrangement: sixty acres on the west side of Harrington Road. Again, the parcel was too small; Wagner told Groark the only way to make the donation work would be to acquire the seventy-five-acre William Farris dairy farm and a couple of nearby allotments. Firestone officials called the donation off and nothing was heard for more than a year.

Then one day Groark walked into the park district's office and told Wagner: "I'm in a hole, and you need to help get me out of it." It seems that Groark had been trying to buy the Farris farm, but Farris believed Groark was scouting for the tire company, not for the park district. Farris refused to sell. Wagner confirmed to Farris that the land would be used as a park, at which point the farmer sold his farm for $20,000. The rubber company cut the check.

With the Farris farm, the purchase of another approximately thirty-one acres and a donation of eighty-four acres from Firestone (which included a couple of holes from the Firestone public golf course), the Firestone Metropolitan Park was created and dedicated in August 1941.

True to form, Wagner had already laid the groundwork for the park, which was to include a skating pond and another CCC-built shelter. Little did anyone know that a brewing war in Europe would bring all these grand plans to a halt in less than six months.

Still, in only sixteen years, the Akron Metropolitan Park District grew from a .176-acre triangle to six distinct parks totaling more than two thousand acres. That would have to be good enough for a quarter century; no new parks would appear in the system for another twenty-five years.

CHAPTER THREE

Making Places for People

I**T TOOK EQUAL PORTIONS** of nerve, bluster and a taste for jigsaw puzzles to assemble the land needed to give the parks a good start. But that kind of hard work was only the beginning. The land was being bought for the people of Summit County. Parks had to be developed to make good on their promise.

Buying into the Olmsteds' vision gave a clear starting point. The Boston landscapers thought the area was ideally suited to parkways linking various important vistas. With Seiberling's donation of land along Sand Run, which he had already developed into a bridle trail for his guests at Stan Hywet, the time was ripe to build a parkway, handily following the bridle trail route and the stream that gives the valley its name.

However, even in the late 1920s, it took money to build roads, and the park board had precious little to spare out of the taxes left over from the larger county budget. The board needed its own, dedicated source of income. The need for a levy was clear, but the board did not act until Wagner forced the issue.

It was the summer of 1928, and as far as anyone could tell, life was good in Akron and Summit County. The time was ripe for a fall levy campaign, but all of the commissioners were out of town. The August filing deadline for ballot issues was fast approaching. Wagner was blunt: "I took it upon myself to break the law. It wasn't the first time, and it probably won't be the last."

Wagner approached James Corey, the head of the Summit County Board of Elections, with language in hand for the November ballot, and a proposal. He told Corey: "I'm going to give you a copy of a resolution passed by the board. One [board member] is in California, the other is in Canada, and I don't know where the third one is.

"Take this resolution. You can lock it in your desk. When the commissioners get back, if they don't like it, you can take it out of your desk and we can make a fire with it. If they go for it, it will have been submitted before the deadline."

The young park executive had solved one problem but he had created another for himself once the commissioners returned to town.

"Boy, did they go through the roof. They really let me have it," Wagner said of the commissioners' reaction to his overstepping his authority. After some conversation, he left the room so commissioners could talk among themselves and choose a course of action. They called him back shortly.

"They said if you can get this done this way, you go ahead and do it," he recalled. So in the fall of 1928, with little more than a few dollars— some of it his own—and women from the Akron Garden Club wearing white sashes emblazoned with "Vote for the Metropolitan Park Levy" strolling near polling places, the voters approved the board's first .1-mill levy. That first year it brought in about $52,000.

Bridle trail in Sand Run Metropolitan Park, August 1929; it was used by F.A. Seiberling's guests

Park vehicles on Sand Run Parkway, 1930, two years after the district's first levy was approved by voters

Now work could begin in earnest. There already were plans to build Sand Run Parkway between Merriman Road and the ford. There were plans to build picnic areas at Old Portage and Wadsworth Camp, including installing waterlines from a natural spring on the north slope of Sand Run Valley and to remodel an old hunting lodge donated by Emil Gammeter into Coon Hollow Camp, which would eventually be used for camping and outdoor education programs for schoolchildren.

Trails had to be first on the agenda. There were plans to build up to five miles of nature trails throughout the steep and lush ravines in Sand Run, but the board took the path of least resistance. The first paths would be for horses and riders.

It was a logical choice. There already were miles of bridle trails that Wagner had built for Stan Hywet when he had been working for Warren Manning. Those only needed some repair. There was great interest in bridle trails from members of the Portage Riding Club, located at Harbel Manor, the estate of Harvey S. Firestone, who had recently purchased a stable of ten thoroughbred horses.

Wagner approached Firestone Tire & Rubber Co. officials with a proposal to develop the trail. If Firestone and other riders would put up $10,000, the park board would provide the labor and materials. Firestone wrote a check for half that cost, and members of the riding club pledged the remainder. The trail was refurbished and opened.

What seemed like a common-sense bargain turned into nothing but a headache. As chronicled in park board minutes and copious correspondence, bridle trails simply created opportunities for frequent clashes between horseback riders and other park users. There were no trails for hikers, so people and horses often found themselves on the same paths. Riders often strayed from the trails, galloping through picnic grounds and tearing up newly seeded turf. The area was quite rural, with more than one dairy farm adjacent to the park still in business. Farm gates were left open and livestock would wander onto park grounds, adding roundups to caretakers' duties.

It would be unfair to stereotype all the riders as arrogant, but there was plenty of hubris to spare. Riders routinely ignored caretakers' requests to stay on the bridle path. After pedestrian nature trails were built, horses frequently strayed onto the less-used hiking trails. When riding became more widely popular and stables began to rent horses by the hour, problems only got worse. Park violation records contain report after report of damage caused by riders galloping on nature trails or in picnic areas. Wagner's superintendent of maintenance, Forrest B. Coup, was on hand to witness a park ranger being browbeaten by a rider who had broken the rules: "Do you know who I am? I'll get you fired." Even Wagner's daughter, caught riding off-trail, huffed to a caretaker: "I could get you fired. Do you know who my father is?" One rider even went to jail for sixty days for beating a farmer who objected to the man and horse crossing his land.

The unkindest cut came when the Portage Riding Club fell short of its $5,000 pledge. The Depression hit everyone hard. Although the park board had kept its bargain by providing the labor and materials to build

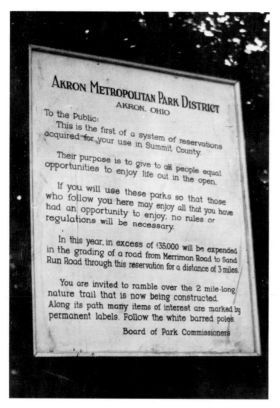

AKRON METROPOLITAN PARK DISTRICT
AKRON, OHIO

To the Public:

This is the first of a system of reservations acquired for your use in Summit County.

Their purpose is to give to all people equal opportunities to enjoy life out in the open.

If you will use these parks so that those who follow you here may enjoy all that you have had an opportunity to enjoy, no rules or regulations will be necessary.

In this year, in excess of (35,000 will be expended in the grading of a road from Merriman Road to Sand Run Road through this reservation for a distance of 3 miles.

You are invited to ramble over the 2 mile-long nature trail that is now being constructed. Along its path many items of interest are marked by permanent labels. Follow the white barred poles.

Board of Park Commissioners

In 1929, park commissioners posted this sign to notify visitors about the Sand Run Parkway project.

the bridle trail, its effort was never fully repaid. When sending a check for half of the promised amount, contrite Firestone executive Russell Happoldt wrote Wagner: "It seems this year it is easier to get promises than cash."

Horses and riders may have been the first, but they were far from the most important users of the park. Picnic areas were full from the first day Sand Run opened in April 1930, requiring picnic tables, metal trash baskets and iron stoves for cooking out.

Nature trails were soon sprouting among the trees and ravines, aided by Western Reserve Academy teacher William Vinal, who persuaded his summer school students to supply the labor for a five-mile oval trail in Sand Run while the parkway was under construction. Such help was crucial. Building a road through nearly virgin forest cost $45,000—most of the first year's levy income.

Sand Run was by far the largest of the park board's holdings, but the same kinds of things were happening at Furnace Run, Goodyear Heights and the Gorge. Once in park board hands, the newly acquired acreage had to be returned to a more natural state. That meant transplanting thousands of trees from the nursery at Old Portage (also part of Sand Run). In 1929 and 1930, park maintenance crews transplanted more than eighty-three thousand trees to its other holdings and even were able to lend five thousand seedlings to Camp Manatoc, the Boy Scout camp near Peninsula.

Workers tow balled trees down Sand Run Parkway, March 1931

Still, commissioners had bigger plans for development, wanting shelters and other facilities for park users. Beginning in 1930, proposed park board budgets reflected this desire. There were plans for two shelters at Furnace Run, one for Goodyear Heights, one at the Gorge and two at Sand Run. However, post-stock market crash budgets fell far short of being able to do much more than patrol, plant and maintain.

Even worse than stagnant budgets, Sand Run was faced with a far more serious problem: raw sewage in its namesake waterway. Part of the problem came from Montrose Dairy, located on the north rim of the Sand Run valley. Operators dumped its waste into a culvert north of the park, and that culvert emptied into the creek west of Sand Run Road. The other bore an ironic connection to Wagner.

Fairlawn Heights, F.A. Seiberling's upscale suburban development, was growing, perhaps too quickly. The homes did not have adequate sewer service, and raw sewage from those homes was flowing directly into Sand Run. Besides being a health hazard, Wagner had lofty hopes for the park, whose users, he said, "have every right to expect that the stream should be fit to bathe in."

Still, Fairlawn Heights residents weren't eager to take on the expense of a sewer system. They tried to stall upgrading sewer service until Akron annexed the area, which would occur in 1932. However, the problems were so serious that, in 1931, the county agreed to build a trunk sewer line along the parkway to connect with the city's new 1928 treatment plant at Botzum.

The sewer line helped for a time, but even a casual reading of the meticulous notes taken by park staff during sewer construction—Wagner's education included engineering—hint at future problems. The notes are full of complaints about inadequate fill, poor-quality joints and contractors ignoring park inspectors. That laid the groundwork for a continuing struggle over sewer problems in Sand Run. By 1945, the county sewers had broken, again dumping raw sewage into Sand Run. And Montrose Dairy would have to go out of business, sometime in the 1940s, to end the use of Sand Run as its farm waste sewer.

Despite those serious insults to Sand Run, the Depression was a far more serious threat to the entire park system. Despite passage of the levy, housing values were plummeting, taking property taxes with them. Wagner took two hefty pay cuts. Laborers were reduced to half-time or less. The board made Goodyear Heights its priority for spending because it was the only metropolitan park in the city and it was well used by the people who lived nearby, mostly Goodyear workers. That would include using the board's dwindling cash to buy adjoining land so that the hemmed-in park could grow. With an annual budget of $44,000 and three other parks to develop and maintain, even those priorities had to be modest.

The Salvation Army provided some help in the form of relief workers, men who had asked for financial help and who agreed to work in return. Park dump trucks hauled workers to and from primitive job sites almost as often as they hauled material. The focus on Goodyear Heights made more than geographic sense. Workers were plentiful in the neighborhood and could walk to work. Wagner even bought the workers' lunches if the Salvation Army didn't want to wait for the county auditor to certify their income so they would qualify for free meals.

All that would soon change. Franklin Delano Roosevelt's election in 1932 was the salvation of the parks. FDR did not wait for his inauguration to get to work. By March 1933, Congress had passed the Emergency Conservation Work Act, which created the Civilian Conservation Corps. It would focus on building and maintaining public parks.

It could have been a bureaucratic nightmare. The Department of Labor was in charge of choosing the participants, the Army in charge of training, feeding and sheltering them, and the Departments of Agriculture and Interior supervised their work. It turned out to be a boon to everyone concerned.

The CCC gave boys and young men work building needed facilities for public entities such as state and national parks. Although metropolitan parks were not state parks, federal officials saw the opportunity that park districts offered for employing out-of-work Americans. It didn't hurt that park officials, led by Wagner, were lobbying loudly for a flexible definition of parks.

When Wagner told the board about the CCC, commissioners told him to go after at least one, if not more work camps. By this time, the state legislature was getting ready to give Virginia Kendall State Park to the park district to manage. Wagner was told to try for a CCC camp at the Boston Township site. He proved a master at threading bureaucratic needles. Not only did he win two camps, but he also was able to get them running quickly. By August 1933, the first CCC camps were being built at Sand Run and Virginia Kendall, even before the state turned over management to the park district. Recruits arrived in Peninsula in December. As well, several of the district's employees, including its stenographer, were moved onto the Civil Works Administration payroll, giving the district financial breathing room while still getting its work done.

Such fiscal maneuvers benefited everyone. Although partisan politics was kept at a minimum when it came to operating the CCC, it wasn't entirely absent.

Tracy Douglas, the commissioner who replaced F.A. Seiberling, also worked as a supervisor for the CCC. In 1935, Harold Ickes, head of the Interior Department, tried to fire Douglas because of the potential conflict of interest in having a commissioner approve projects on which he might be working. Wagner intervened, telling Ickes that Douglas' CCC work did not occur in the parks. The firing was rescinded, but Douglas was assigned a CCC camp at the state forestry department in southern Ohio. He remained a board member until 1936, when he resigned.

Because the park district had planned its development before the Depression, it was ready to start. Plans included shelters in each of Sand Run, Furnace Run, the Gorge and Goodyear Heights. It included constructing trails. It also included paving Sand Run Parkway with something other than gravel. It included digging ponds for fishing and ice skating.

The CCC arrived at the same time Deep Lock Quarry was donated to the park board. Although it would be several decades before the land along the Ohio & Erie Canal would be developed for recreation, it was immediately pressed into service supplying stone for the shelters, for steps to negotiate Virginia Kendall's steep pathways and for other public construction projects requiring the area's signature Berea sandstone while teaching young men stone quarrying.

CCC barracks under construction, November 1933

The Depression-era program helped the district exceed even its own most ambitious plans by the time the CCC ended in 1942. Nine years after recruits first arrived, nearly $1 million worth of buildings and other attractions existed in the Akron Metropolitan Park District, and more than $750,000 had been sent home by the recruits to their families. Sand Run had shelters at Wadsworth and Mingo camps, and new trails, bridges and fords. Goodyear Heights had a new shelter, as did the Gorge and Furnace Run. Both Furnace Run and Virginia Kendall had new dams that created swimming lakes and new bathhouses. Virginia Kendall's three new shelters— The Ledges, The Octagon and Happy Days—all were built with American wormy chestnut, salvaged from the local forests after a killing blight nearly wiped it out. Today, those wormy-chestnut shelters (now managed by Cuyahoga Valley National Park) are historic artifacts. Generations of visitors

CCC workers at Mingo Pavilion in Sand Run Metropolitan Park, April 1935

to Virginia Kendall also enjoyed the toboggan chutes near Kendall Lake, first built by the CCC and later expanded and improved by the park district.

But the CCC gave something even more important to the parks than physical assets. In 1934, Forrest B. Coup was hired into the CCC as a blacksmith and tool sharpener. He proved so invaluable that the park district hired him as a field maintenance supervisor a year later. He would serve as superintendent of maintenance until Wagner retired in 1958, and as director until 1963, when he retired after twenty-eight years of service.

The CCC also offered area residents a visible reason to support their parks. The young men of the Civilian Conservation Corps not only built the shelters people used, they also attended schools as part of the training program. They became members of the community.

Steps to Mingo Pavilion restrooms, April 1935

There were other plans that never quite made it. In 1936, Summit County began leasing its property between Merriman Road and Portage Path, once designated for a county hospital, to the park district to build an amphitheater by the Works Progress Administration. The plans were ready by 1937 but stalled. Unlike the CCC, WPA projects required a 20 percent local match. Park income had barely grown; the 1938 budget was $45,500. There would be no amphitheater. And there was bureaucracy. U.S. Rep. Dow Harter, a key player in supporting the district's CCC programs, received this observation from Wagner about a local WPA official: "No violent animosity between us, but he seems to have peculiar ideas about running his branch of public affairs. I know I could not get away with such deportment. I wouldn't want to, for I have found after some

A man sits in Wadsworth Shelter in Sand Run Metropolitan Park, 1930s

ten or fifteen years of this work that I can come pretty close to public approval by treating *everybody alike*" (emphasis Wagner's).

When Firestone Metropolitan Park was added to the district's holdings in the summer of 1941, plans were ready for the CCC to dig a fishing pond and to build a shelter and trails. In addition, the busy park district was run out of a fourth floor office in the County Courthouse. If the board could persuade county commissioners to sell the county hospital land in Sand Run, there would be more than enough land for a new headquarters at Merriman and Merridge (now Treaty Line) Road. The CCC even developed plans for such a building.

None of those plans would go forward. Preparation for war had already strained supplies of recruits and material. If Pearl Harbor was the beginning of World War II, it was the end of the CCC and of the small building boom that had taken Summit County's park district far beyond its pre-Depression dreams.

The war caused new problems, not the least of which was finding lifeguards for the two lakes the CCC had built at Virginia Kendall and Furnace Run. Even if there had been enough lifeguards, they would have had trouble getting to either far-flung location because of gasoline and tire rationing. The district kept only Virginia Kendall's lake open for swimming, angering Richfield-area residents, who had just celebrated the opening of Brushwood Lake in 1941. In fact, Virginia Kendall's season was cut short that first year of war because of severe rationing.

Brushwood Lake remained closed during the war. That didn't stop people from using the lake illegally, to the point where the board told Richfield to hire its own lifeguards and pay the board $100. It would open again after the war, and be used by various groups, such as Red Raiders and the American Red Cross for swimming lessons. However, silt would prove its undoing. Park staff continually tried to keep the lake free of soil runoff caused by increasing development in Brecksville, where storm runoff flowed into the Furnace Run watershed. Finally, after the Ohio Turnpike was built over Furnace Run's north shoulder in the mid-1950s, it would effectively end the use of Brushwood Lake for swimming.

After the war, some stalled projects were put back in play, most notably the development of Firestone Metropolitan Park. Staff filled in the swamp where one of the main parking lots is located and leveled a hill for a shelter. Wells provided plenty of clear water for the new building.

This time, of course, there would be no CCC to build it, but in the post-war years, the board was financially able to handle the shelter's $90,000 price tag, "much more money than we'd spent in all the facilities we'd built up to that point," Wagner recalled in 1971. The board hired the architectural firm of Good and Wagner (no relation to Harold S. Wagner) and proceeded.

The board took a risk, building a year-round structure of brick and reinforced concrete with a basement and heating plant. It would be different in appearance and potential use from anything the board had attempted to this point, but commissioners felt it was necessary because of development in the southeastern part of Summit County.

Construction proceeded smoothly until it came to the selection of brick to face it. Because Firestone Tire had helped in the purchase of the park, its officials felt they should have a say in how the building looked. Their taste clashed with that of the board, particularly Mark Kindig, who was chairman while the shelter was under construction.

The board had traveled throughout Northeast Ohio to research brick. After looking at and rejecting about fifty different kinds, they had decided to use what was known as sand-finished, Cleveland common brick. As Wagner recalled, one morning an engineer from Firestone came out to the building site where some of the brick had been used in a sample wall. While he said nothing at the time, the engineer's visit resulted in a call to Wagner later that day saying that Firestone officials did not like the color. They were "very much interested in using the same kind of brick used in building the last of Firestone's buildings in South Akron—yellow brick."

Because it was a public building, board members felt the decision was theirs. Firestone officials believed just as strongly that their contribution entitled them to final say. The board and the company were at an impasse. While park board members Henry Metzger and Walton Woodling did not really care, Kindig and architect Ab Good were adamant. Work was stopped; bricklayers sat idle at least two weeks.

Then Kindig traveled west on business without leaving word where he was going. Firestone sent people in search of Kindig, and they finally found him. Wagner got a call.

"With no dearth of profanity, he [Kindig] said 'Let them have what they want. I'm sick of it.'"

As he had done with the board's first levy in 1928, Wagner took matters into his own hands. He reminded Kindig of the architect's wishes and then said: "If you don't mind, I'll go ahead on my own, and I'll order

Virginia Kendall bathhouse construction by CCC workers, April 1936

Workers build picnic tables in the work shop, Sand Run Metropolitan Park, July 1935

the brick and have it delivered on the job. I'll tell the guy to go ahead and lay brick, the brick that we want."

Kindig's response was terse but supportive: "Anything you do, I'll go with you."

In the end, Firestone officials "just loved" the shelter and the brick, so much so that they wanted the company's logo, a large script *F* engraved on the shelter's broad chimney. The board thought otherwise. In the end the company settled for a bronze plaque inside the shelter acknowledging its role in the development of that park.

Another project stalled by World War II would go forward far more slowly. The county hospital property in Sand Run, which had been targeted for a new park headquarters, was mired in county politics. Despite special legislation to ease the transfer of land between the county and the park board, the park district was forced to continue leasing the land—for $1 a year—until 1975, when the park district finally bought the land and began building its present headquarters on Treaty Line Road.

In the meantime, the county courthouse was filling up, and the Akron Bar Association asked all agencies not directly involved in court business to move to make room for the Grand Jury. In 1950, park district offices moved nearby to South Broadway, although commissioners often met at the West Market Street offices of commissioner Joseph Thomas, a Firestone lawyer.

Clearly, the district needed larger offices. At the same time, its ever-popular Goodyear Heights Metropolitan Park was in need of a new, larger shelter. It seemed two needs could be met with one project. First, however, the park's wartime-era Victory Gardens had to go. As with cities all over the country, such gardens had served a vital role in helping people grow their own food during World War II. Both Goodyear and Firestone rubber companies had worked with the park district to offer land for workers and their families. Firestone's program ended shortly after the war ended.

Crews pour concrete for the shelter in Firestone Metropolitan Park, March 1948

On the other hand. Goodyear's gardens on the former McKay property, near the corner of Darrow Road and Newton Street, had become so popular that commissioners had a hard time closing them. Each time they voted to end the garden program, a nearly annual vote after 1950, intrepid staff at Goodyear would first enlist gardeners and then present commissioners with the request to extend the gardening program "just one more season." Goodyear had effectively turned the gardens into a free employee benefit.

It was hard to say no. The program was popular. Wagner judged contests for the largest of different kinds of produce and graded gardeners on their technique.

Finally, pressure to find new space won. Plans for a new shelter in hand, commissioners halted the gardening program in 1953 and began work on the new shelter on Newton Street in Goodyear Heights Metropolitan Park and a new recreation field behind the shelter.

The $154,000 shelter at Goodyear Heights would be the largest ever attempted by the park district on its own. It would dwarf the Firestone

The completed shelter in Firestone Metropolitan Park, 1948

shelter, with two wings to accommodate groups, full kitchens in each, a basement and, after some argument from commissioner Hezzleton Simmons, a second floor. It was into that space that the park district would move its headquarters. Appropriately, the shelter was named the Charles Goodyear Memorial Shelter, after the inventor of vulcanization and the tire company's namesake. It was dedicated Aug. 11, 1957. It came in on time and under budget.

If building the shelter was a high point for the district, a downswing was lurking. An anti-park contingent in the state legislature had slipped a quirk in state law requiring two-thirds voter approval for levies. In 1955, even though a majority of voters approved the district's levy, it failed to meet the two-thirds requirement. After several other park districts suffered similar technical defeats, the law was changed back. But by that time voters had soured, rejecting levies in 1957 and 1958.

Also in 1955, the state announced plans to impound the Tuscarawas River near Firestone Metropolitan Park. At first, the board's concern focused on relocating Harrington Road and building parking spaces for the shelter and on Warner Road. Those issues proved minor. The new dam raised the water table, eventually flooding the shelter. The board was forced to raise the basement floor four feet and relocate all utilities.

Goodyear Memorial Shelter, 1957

While the state eventually paid for the damage, the board spent money it could ill-afford keeping the shelter open.

The Charles Goodyear Memorial Shelter would be the last structure built by the board for many years. By 1959, the park district was barely able to operate. Half the district's workers were laid off in 1958. Wagner, who would retire before the next levy, had plans to work only a skeleton staff to maintain and guard the parks if they were forced to close. The passage of a last-gasp levy in the fall of 1959 kept that from happening.

There was another threat to the parks that would preoccupy the board for the next decade and more. Rapid suburbanization and highway construction would cut deeply into park holdings. The commissioners and staff would face a new threat from runoff and pollution. And, while the Olmsteds did not advocate saving the entire Cuyahoga Valley, these population growth spurts worried park commissioners in both Cuyahoga and Summit counties that the valley that simultaneously separated and connected the two urban counties would disappear. They began to look for ways to save the valley before it disappeared. Thus began a new, desperate push to buy land.

CHAPTER FOUR

Getting People into the Parks

WHEN EVA WILLEN and her extended family showed up for the first Fall Hiking Spree in 1964, they were in the vanguard of what has become one of the nation's oldest and most popular annual outdoor recreation events. Matriarch Eva, seventy-one, complete with apron and button shoes, brought her daughter, two granddaughters and five great-grandchildren to hike the seven inaugural trails. After that, the Fall Hiking Spree became a family affair, and now a fifth generation of Eva Willen's family continues to hike each fall. And given that great-great grandson Adam Stone proposed to his now-wife, Jennifer, on a park trail, it's more than possible that the sixth generation of Eva Willen's family will continue their fall parade.

It has been this way for thousands of people since that fall almost fifty years ago. The hiking spree is a simple idea: Offer people an incentive to strike out on the miles of trails that have been built throughout the park district in the hope that it will bring the parks and people closer.

It was the brainchild of Arthur Wilcox, at the time director-secretary of the park district. It didn't matter that he served the shortest tenure of the district's six directors. His influence—from the hiking spree to the *Green Islands* publication—continues to be felt.

A young Wilcox, fresh from completing his degree in landscape architecture, was first hired in the late 1930s to draw plans for the park's CCC projects. By this time, Forrest B. Coup had been hired from the CCC to run the district's maintenance department. Knowing Wilcox's interest in parks, the detail-oriented Coup did two things. First, he took him under his wing, teaching the young man by example.

"He took me to Virginia Kendall Park one day," Wilcox recalled in a 2003 interview, "and offered me a piece of chewing gum. I flicked the wrapper into a bush. Mr. Coup looked for that wrapper for forty-five minutes. When he found it, he put it in his pocket. I never threw another piece of trash in any park, ever."

The other thing Coup did was order the young architect to survey the boundaries of every park in the district's holdings. This gave Wilcox a personal view of the wealth of natural beauty the district held even at that early point in its history. It was an impression that never left him.

He might have spent years at that job, but World War II intervened. The day after Pearl Harbor, Wilcox applied to be a draftsman at Goodyear Aircraft, having been rejected by the Navy for bad knees. He designed tools for the Corsair and B-26.

After the war, Wilcox returned to the park district for a short time, but soon left to go to Michigan State University, where he created a graduate

Dr. Arthur T. Wilcox

program in outdoor recreation management. For all he knew, the good-byes would be forever.

However, in 1959, he got a call from his old boss, Forrest Coup. Harold Wagner had retired the year before. While Coup had taken over for him, he, too, was ready to retire. When that call came, Wilcox had built a solid reputation with his parks management program. Coup asked him to recommend someone to take over. His old love of the district and the opportunity for hands-on management persuaded Wilcox to take the job himself. He and his family moved back to the Akron area in 1960.

Although he would not officially replace Coup for another three years, Wilcox effectively took the reins immediately as chief landscape engineer and secretary for the district. With the encouragement of park commissioner Forrest Myers, whose passion was acquiring land, Wilcox began to map out areas that the district wanted or needed to buy in the short term to ensure their preservation for public use. Suburbanization was spreading throughout Summit County in the early 1960s, and many parcels, particularly in outlying parks, were threatened by development.

Wilcox also encouraged the publication of a regular newsletter to keep the public up to date on park events. Taking a cue from the Cleveland Metroparks' *Emerald Necklace*, a play on the interconnection of Cuyahoga County's metropolitan parks, Wilcox and Naturalist Bert Szabo named Summit County's newsletter *Green Islands*, its parks sprinkled like islands throughout the county. Along with *Woodland Trails*, which focused specifically on animals and plants in the parks, the publications were immediately successful.

However, Wilcox's most lasting contribution was to be the Fall Hiking Spree, which kicked off in 1964. It remains the country's longest running

Rangers Bob Stephens and Aaron Mitchell with John Kasarda, 1960s

and most successful hiking program. Wilcox called it a spree to give hikers the idea they were doing something fun instead of work.

The hiking spree did not spring from a whim. Wilcox knew from his days walking park boundaries and designing trails for the CCC that the parks, for all their natural beauty, were underused. He wanted to find a way to get people into the parks so they could see and experience what he already knew to be treasures.

There was also another purpose to the spree. Park rangers had an image problem. Because they are required to be certified peace officers, with badges, guns and arrest powers, rangers were seen more as enforcers than helpers. Park users did not feel welcome, but the spree turned rangers into guides, telling hikers more about the parks.

Working with John Kasarda, who had replaced Coup as head of maintenance, Wilcox created a template that remains in place to this day. He

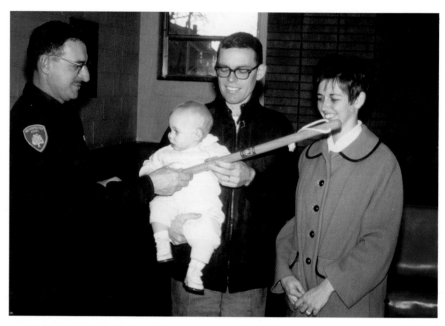

Dave and Nancy Reinhart and their son, Rodd, receive a hiking staff from Naturalist Bert Szabo in 1968

mapped out a total of twelve miles along seven trails in the district's six parks to be included in the first hiking spree. Each hiker had to have a form signed by a ranger.

One of the inaugural spree trails ran through Deep Lock Quarry. Although the district had owned the land since 1934, it had never been open to the public as a park until 1964.

As an incentive, Wilcox and Kasarda planned to give out hiking staffs made of small saplings cut from the parks to all Summit County residents who completed the seven hikes. They thought too small. By the end of the first spree, over fifteen hundred people had earned hiking staffs, including Wilcox, whose daughter, Anita, persuaded her parents to hit the trails so they could all earn their own staffs.

The overwhelming response presented a problem, because Wilcox and Kasarda were loath to cut that many saplings. Bob Butcher of the

Butcher Construction Co. brought a rescue in the form of enough mop handles to give to all the successful hikers.

Today, each county resident completing the spree for the first time still receives a hiking staff.

But what could the parks offer repeat hikers in future sprees? Naturalist Szabo, who led many of the guided spree hikes on Sunday afternoons, suggested offering a metal shield to veteran hikers that could be attached to their staffs. That idea came from a park district in Germany.

There would be small changes in future years. Since 1971, hikers have been offered a menu of up to fourteen trails from which they choose eight. In 2009, the Hiker's Choice option was added, allowing participants to hike any one trail in the district, whether or not it was on the spree form.

In 1972, a nine-year-old girl who was not a Summit County resident completed the spree, only to be denied a hiking staff. Commissioner Forrest Myers gave the girl a staff that year, but it would take another twenty-five years for the policy to change. In 1997, non-residents who hiked the spree were offered a staff for $10, and over two hundred non-Summit hikers claimed their awards. Now, non-resident veterans pay $5 for a shield; first-timers pay $10 for their staff.

Not that non-residents weren't hiking before 1997. Far from it. A hiking staff made its way to Australia's state of New South Wales via Colin Ducker, who hiked the second-annual spree and received a staff while living in Barberton as an exchange student. Forty-five years later, Akron native Margaret Emily Lumsden returned home from New Zealand to complete the spree. She finds a leisurely walk through the woods to be a great way to catch up on hometown news.

Many hikers were like Mrs. Willen, who at seventy-one didn't seem to be the average hiking age. She had plenty of company, such as Emery Hanes, who was seventy-nine in 1964 and completed the first spree. He did not claim a staff because, as he told an *Akron Beacon Journal* reporter,

A 1965 Fall Hiking Spree
certificate of achievement
belonging to Bill Barnes,
who has completed every
Fall Hiking Spree to date.
In 1964, first-year hikers
received a hiking staff.
Commemorative shields
were introduced the
second year

Shields from
1965 and 2011

In 2008, eighteen of the twenty-one hikers who had completed the Fall Hiking Spree in each of the first forty-five years posed for this picture at Goodyear Heights Metro Park.

he didn't need anything to hang onto. Hanes, a maintenance worker for the park district, on his third career after stints at Goodrich and Standard Oil, estimated he had walked about 150,000 miles in his life. Or like J. Luther Reiter, who tried for five years to complete the spree. He finally succeeded in 1970, when he was eighty-seven.

Although similar programs in other districts have not persisted, Summit County's has built a loyal following. In 2008, the forty-fifth spree included twenty-one hikers who had completed all forty-four previous sprees, including Szabo, who retired from the park district in 1991, but has continued not only to hike the fall spree, but contribute thousands of volunteer hours.

Szabo seems to have a handle on what has made the spree so enduring. "Once people get started, they can't seem to stop. They brag about it, bring their friends and relatives along. It becomes a challenge," he said during an interview.

No one understands the concept of challenge better than Eileene Ball of Clinton who endured most of the 1994 spree—her thirtieth—in a body cast as she healed from cancer surgery on her spine and ribs. The cast did not come off until October, so she hiked the beginning of the spree that year in her cast. Maybe challenges are just in her blood. She recalled a picnic at Goodyear Heights Metro Park that she and several of her co-workers from First National Bank enjoyed despite six inches of snow on the ground and the picnic table. Mrs. Ball, eighty-two in 2008, said she would hike as long as she could, committing to five-year stretches at a time.

For some people, hiking is more than a once-a-year passion. That would be someone like Nancy Grof of Barberton, seventy-nine, who found the first hiking spree so exciting that she and several other people immediately formed the Akron Metro Parks Hiking Club, which also turned forty-eight in 2011. Besides having perfect attendance at all hiking sprees, she estimates she has hiked at least fifteen thousand miles with that group. She is the only charter member of the hiking club remaining.

Jennifer Hoffman, who began hiking the trails as a fourteen-year-old with her parents in 1964, continues the tradition with neighborhood friends. She is on her second hiking staff because the first became too crowded with shields.

But perhaps George Figel has the most at stake in continuing to hike each fall. The retiree recalled that he didn't feel his usual energetic self while hiking the trails in 1990, so he told his doctor. That piece of information led to double bypass surgery, but he was back for the 1991 spree.

"The hiking spree was a real life saver," Figel said. He continues to hike, but in the mornings, as he volunteers for the Red Cross transportation service and the Bloodmobile in the afternoons.

Bill Barnes notes that the park district has grown since he started hiking the spree. It did not include Silver Creek Metro Park or the Furnace Run Daffodil Trail. He especially enjoys Hampton Hills, added in 1964. He now leads regular walks with his fellow residents at Sumner on Ridgewood. Eighty-four as the 2008 hiking spree kicked off, Barnes also noted he was the youngest participant in his group, with the exception of the woman who drove the bus.

However, even as the hiking spree remained a district focal point, it became clear there were many people for whom even a casual stroll on some of the district's trails was impossible. Many of the spree's first participants were aging and wanted a less taxing event. Others would never be able to hike the trails included in the spree's trails buffet.

Phyllis Boerner, who previously had worked for the park district in varying roles and who had helped found the group Friends of Metro Parks, was by 2004 head of communications for United Disability Services. She started talking with park staff about a hiking event for people with disabilities. At the same time, officials from Summa Health System had approached Susan Fairweather, then the chief of marketing and communication for the park district, seeking an opportunity to sponsor something like the hiking spree to emphasize the importance of fitness for people of all abilities.

With the nub of an idea and support to get it started, all that remained was a way to link it to the popular fall event. Naturalist Maureen McGinty found it in a name: Spree For All. The new series combines with the Fall Hiking Spree to give hikers signature bookend events in unsurpassed natural settings.

Spree For All's template remains similar to the fall event: Complete five hikes from a menu of selected trails between May 1 and June 30 each year. Everyone who completes the spree receives a commemorative pin, lanyard and pouch. Each subsequent year, participants receive a new pin to add to their lanyards.

On May 1, 2004, former naturalist Bert Szabo, with Ohio Governor Bob Taft, led the first-ever public Spree For All hike at Goodyear Heights Metro Park.

Spree For All participants who hike five times receive a commemorative pin; pictured are pins from the inaugural year through 2011.

The program is not as large as the Fall Hiking Spree, which officials say eleven to twelve thousand people complete each year. Spree For All sees about two thousand hikers earn awards annually.

Gail Wilmott, editor of *Kaleidoscope* magazine for United Disability Services and who uses a motorized wheelchair, tested two of the trails before the inaugural Spree For All. Her words, most apt for those not often included in outside activities, included those Summit County residents who have taken a hike in the woods during one kind of spree or another:

"It's just nice to get an opportunity to be outside and get on a trail," she said.

CHAPTER FIVE

Going Natural

Take a walk through the Metro Parks with a naturalist, and what once was a beautiful collection of trees and plants begin to dress up in names and stories. Naturalists are known as environmental educators and the folks who read the pages of the woods to visitors, who tell the stories about these parks, who help visitors understand and appreciate the wealth that is open space.

This integral component of the park district got its start in the wooded nooks of Sand Run Metropolitan Park, where Shady Hollow Pavilion now sits. Emil Gammeter and his brother John, local leaders and park proponents, owned a small hunting cabin in what had once been known as the Portage Game Preserve. They donated it to the fledgling park district, and even before Sand Run Parkway opened in 1929, the small remodeled cabin became known as Coon Hollow Camp.

Gammeter's Lodge, February 1929

In 1931 it served as the outdoor schoolroom for small groups of children taught by William Vinal, who also taught at Western Reserve Academy and for the Cleveland Board of Education. It was part of a broader vision articulated by Maude Milar, a teacher and one of the first three park commissioners. While avidly interested in forestry and an important member of local women's clubs, her passion was the educational value of parks. After she retired from the board, she told her former colleagues in a letter:

> "If I have aided one iota in creating favorable public opinion for park service, I trust the Board will remember it only in their promotion of the one purpose uppermost in my mind from my earliest teaching days: that is, trained nature work in the outdoors for the pupils of our public schools."

It was an ideal place to teach children about wildlife and plants. The relatively unspoiled woods teemed with native trees and wildflowers and, given its former life as a game preserve, wildlife abounded. Indeed, John

Western Reserve Academy field trip to Coon Hollow Camp, July 1930

Gammeter often pleaded with H.S. Wagner to allow hunting for "pest animals," such as weasels and fox, who were decimating the woods of the quail and partridge he and his brother had released there. In a fit of pique, Wagner allowed hunting during one year to give proponents a chance to prove how overrun the park was with fox. The story is the hunters bagged one.

At about the same time, the Akron Garden Club invited A.B. Brooks of West Virginia University to talk about trails. A nationally recognized forester, he was heralded for designing the trails at the popular Oglebay State Park in Wheeling, West Virginia. Brooks' guided nature hikes in Sand Run proved popular enough that Wagner continued the practice, giving similar guided tours to Akron Public Schools students. The success of this program prompted the board to invest in five miles of nature trails in Sand Run.

Children splashing at Virginia Kendall, August 1938

But Vinal's day camp at Coon Hollow proved to be the seed with the deepest roots. In 1933, after four years of working with students—his Western Reserve Academy students had helped build Sand Run's nature trails—his program moved to Virginia Kendall Park after the park board took control of the former Hayward Kendall estate. For several years, it was housed in the Truxell Road home that had been used by Kendall's caretaker, Howard Dittoe, who remained with the land after Kendall died and his land was transferred to the state. Dittoe was hired first by the state of Ohio and then by the park district as caretaker at Virginia Kendall.

Although the Civilian Conservation Corps would officially name its weekly newsletter *Happy Days*, after the upbeat FDR campaign theme song, the song came to life for hundreds of Akron "playground" children, so called because they were encouraged to play in school yards built for them by the Works Progress Administration instead of the city's streets.

As early as 1934, children boarded buses at their schools in the afternoon Monday through Friday and rode the bumpy East River Road (roughly following the course of today's Akron-Peninsula Road) to Virginia Kendall.

Under the supervision of staff from the Akron Board of Education and Akron Recreation Commission, the children spent the afternoon hiking or playing games. They ate a supper they brought themselves—the children supplied their own food for all three meals at camp—with milk supplied by an Akron men's service organization called the Exchange Club. The camp was not co-ed. One week the girls attended three days of camp and boys the other two. Another week the roles were reversed. After a campfire the children slept overnight in a tent attached to the Dittoe house, went swimming in the CCC-built lake in the morning, ate lunch and then were bused home in the afternoon. This process was repeated five times a week each summer. For many kids it was their only exposure to something other than city streets.

In 1939, Happy Days moved to its present site on State Route 303, after the CCC built a shelter dedicated for use as a summer camp for children. Situated near the Boy Scouts' Camps Manatoc and Butler, it also became the summer home of the area Girl Scouts, which held day camps at Happy Days later in the 1930s and eventually used it for overnight camping.

A seed of a different sort was planted during those days at Virginia Kendall. Helen Sullivan, a teacher with a master's degree from Akron University, was the popular adult who ran the girls' Happy Days camp at both Coon Hollow and Virginia Kendall. Besides being trained in physical education, she had a special quality the kids loved.

"I put all the worms on the hooks," she recalled in a 1997 interview. She also caught the eye of one of the park district's employees. Helen Sullivan recalled waving to Forrest Coup, the young head of maintenance for the parks. As a Board of Education employee, she continued her career teaching physical education at East High School after her tenure at Happy

Happy Days Lodge during construction, November 1938

Days ended during World War II. It did not end the budding romance. Forrest Coup and Helen Sullivan married in 1955.

Still, for all the programs the park district sponsored, it did not have one of its staff members whose only job was nature education. Wagner, as a trained and passionate horticulturist, served that role very well, but he had his hands full running the parks. Commissioners spent some time in the late 1930s talking about hiring a naturalist, but with a drastic shortfall in park district income during the Depression, the district continued to rely on Wagner's nature-guiding programs at Sand Run supplemented by lectures by local and regional experts. Staff was busy trying to keep up with the physical needs of the parks; there was no one to spare.

In the meantime, Akron kids were still attending Happy Days during the week in the summer, and other groups including newspaper carriers attended on weekends. The district offered the Happy Days programs to Barberton, Cuyahoga Falls and Summit County schools. Very few took advantage of the offer.

In 1943, the war nearly closed down Happy Days Camp. Gasoline and tire rationing had pulled Akron Board of Education buses off the road for anything but the most essential travel. The city of Akron had passed its own recreation tax levy, and balked when the park district asked for program expenses to be paid by the city instead of from the Kendall Trust.

However, Congress had just passed the Lanham Act protecting trademarks, and money from those fees was made available to underwrite the camp. It actually worked out better for the children, because Wagner insisted the money be used to buy food and to hire someone to cook for the children so that they no longer had to bring their own food. In 1944, children were charged $1 for their stay at Happy Days, but changes were clearly coming. The district had to hire its own private bus, and the city pulled out of helping to enroll the children because their own playgrounds were swamped. The Girl Scouts stepped in, keeping the program going through 1946.

Throughout this time, the guiding principle was natural recreation, not man-made.

"Wagner was a purist as well as a naturalist," said Bert Szabo, who was officially named the park district's first naturalist in 1964. "He did not like artificial recreation." Szabo said the Sand Run bridle trails were about as artificial as Wagner could tolerate. To Wagner, the parks, and all that existed within them, served a purpose beyond recreation.

"I believe that in order to properly sell parks to the public that it will be necessary to go one step further just as they have in the national system and provide naturalists to help the users of the parks appreciate and realize the full value of what they are providing for themselves," he wrote to Maude Milar in 1929. He never veered from that vision.

Whether he knew it or not at the time, Szabo's hiring in 1957 was one of Wagner's last—and possibly best—efforts to establish an ongoing naturalist program in the parks before his own retirement in 1958.

It didn't begin quite that directly. Szabo, who has degrees in agriculture and plant pathology from Ohio University, had been let go from his job running the farm at Hudson's Western Reserve Academy in 1955. Rapid development in the northern suburb had caused clashes between the farm and its new residential neighbors. Administrators of the college preparatory school decided to sell the farm, leaving Szabo out of work with a growing family to support. Summit County Probate Judge Dean F. May, for whom Szabo did odd jobs around the judge's Hudson home, suggested Szabo talk with Wagner. Perhaps he sensed the two men had a lot in common.

As Szabo recalled of their August 1957 meeting: "He [Wagner] brought me in. He was quite congenial. He put me through the ropes, asked why I wanted the job, names of plants. We talked about horticulture. Then he asked me when I could start work. It was pouring down rain at the time, and I told him my raincoat and boots were in the car."

Szabo started work as a laborer in Sand Run that following Monday, and was made caretaker of Goodyear Heights Metropolitan Park within two weeks. There wasn't a job he couldn't do, from running a bulldozer to wielding a chain saw. He was sworn in as a ranger in 1958. Still, while his job title did not change for several more years, he was groomed almost immediately as the park district's naturalist, attending in 1958 the newly created nature interpretation program at Bradford Woods, Indiana University's outdoor education center. Getting in on the ground floor helped Szabo to shape the future of nature interpretation as an integral part of all park management. Up to that time, the only interpreters regularly employed by parks worked for the National Park Service.

Szabo remained in the dual post, overseeing Goodyear Heights and developing a nature-guiding program for schools, for several more years. In truth, he wore many hats. In 1963, Director Art Wilcox asked Szabo to list the number of jobs he did for the district. Szabo's list numbered twenty-two different tasks, including writing nature articles and running the offset press for *Green Islands* and *Woodland Trails*, two publications started by Wilcox and Szabo. Finally, in 1964, Wilcox whittled that monstrous list to one by creating the post of chief naturalist, a job Szabo held until his retirement in 1991.

The steps at Deep Lock Quarry, circa 1961, before the park was opened and the trail was constructed

During his thirty-three years as naturalist, whether by official title or not, Szabo built a program and a staff that brought the parks closer to people. He started nature walks in 1958. His first winter walk, in 1964, was attended by 150 adults and children. There were classes for school-teachers and others who worked with children. It provided training in nature study and in nature guiding and conservation.

Many of the activities were designed for families. Szabo understood that parents were eager for activities that the entire family could do together. It is hardly a coincidence that of his four children, three have stayed close to the trail their father blazed. One son is a naturalist, one a geologist and a daughter is a teacher in a nature center in Milwaukee. It is also hardly a coincidence that the Fall Hiking Spree started the same year Szabo became chief naturalist. He denies having a hand in its development, giving credit to Wilcox and John Kasarda, then superintendent of maintenance. However, Szabo was an eager participant in the annual

Construction on the millstone-anchored entrance sign to Deep Lock Quarry, 1966

event, often accompanying groups of people as they walked, pointing out interesting details—his passion is birds—along the trail. He has completed every Fall Hiking Spree to date.

Szabo named most of the trails in the park system, including those that had been in the system from the beginning in Furnace Run, the Gorge, Goodyear Heights, Sand Run and Firestone. After he became chief naturalist, the park system added Silver Creek, Hampton Hills, O'Neil Woods and Munroe Falls. And even though it had been owned by the park district since 1934, Deep Lock Quarry opened to the public for the first time during the inaugural Fall Hiking Spree, with Szabo's millstone-anchored sign announcing its location and parking lot. He helped reclaim from choking poison ivy the once barren-rock terrain, complete with open quarry faces and CCC-cut stone so that the public could safely use it. In the meantime, while the park was being prepared, Szabo was learning about quarrying from the mayor of Peninsula, who had worked at the quarry as a young man.

Working with other naturalists who came to work for the park district after he was named chief naturalist—first Carol Anthony Lloyd, then Don Prack and finally Walter Starcher—Szabo began to shape a vision for a nature center where people, particularly children, could have a closer view of wildlife and plants. For a time, the district toyed with the idea of a farm center, located on land off Smith Road acquired in the mid-1960s from the Laughlin family. (The land had once been owned by F.A. Seiberling, too.) A former working dairy farm, the land came with buildings, including a barn that was ideal for a nature classroom. Szabo even found a windmill from a Stow farm and put it up to teach lessons in wind power. It pulled water from an underground cistern and fed it through a trough into a milk house.

With a place to call home, the nature program began to grow. Szabo gained a second naturalist and expanded programs and talks given by his department. They launched an educational program known as School of the Woods, which taught about the wildlife, plants, birds and flowers found in the parks. The open fields at the nature center were particularly well-suited to stargazing, and its abundant plants fed the steady stream of bees ferrying pollen from the fields through a tube with outside access into a visible hive mounted inside the building.

School of the Woods was taught in the barn on the Laughlin property and the nearby house was adapted as a visitors center, filled with exhibits designed and built by Szabo in the basement's carpentry shop. Szabo and the district's landscape architect, Ken Avery, designed and built an herb garden to encourage disabled and visually impaired visitors to touch and smell plants with medicinal, culinary or aromatic properties. The sixty-one-acre site opened to the public as the F.A. Seiberling Nature Center in June 1966. For many years it also was home to rescued owls, raccoons and a skunk.

The late '60s and '70s saw thousands of families, schoolchildren and others visit the center. Eventually, the popular attraction began to show its

The nature center and windmill, 1966

age. As early as 1972, commissioners discussed the need for a larger visitors center, but the district's tax revenues not only were shrinking, owing to a formula built into state law, but commissioners' priorities had changed to buying land in the Cuyahoga Valley. A new center would have to rely on financial help from private individuals, foundations or the federal government. The district did receive a $25,000 planning grant from the Knight Foundation in 1974, the same year its name was changed from the Nature Center to the Naturealm. However, without money to operate the center, commissioners abandoned the idea. Little but the name would change for nearly two decades.

New attractions, such as movies in the park, began at Goodyear Heights Metropolitan Park. When expert photographer Don Prack was hired, School of the Woods expanded to include photography.

In the meantime, the grounds at the Naturealm were taking shape. The former farm was slowly becoming an arboretum, guided by Avery, who had created something similar at his former employer, Cleveland Metroparks. He cut down much of the farm's second-growth forest and

Visitors inspect a turtle at the nature center, August 1969

Naturalist Don Prack works on exhibits for the nature center, October 1968

dredged a new pond. He used soil from the pond to cover the stumps, creating mounds through which walking paths meandered instead of traversing open farm fields. Starting with a donation from an Akron women's service group, WITAN, in memory of its past presidents, the district built a wooden observation deck and began buying specialty trees. Other donations began to roll in.

Szabo persisted in his quest for a larger, more well-equipped visitors center, knowing that the old house was too small for large groups and the office space barely adequate for two naturalists. He and the other naturalist made do, building not only the nature interpretation program for the park district but, because of Szabo's involvement with the national association—serving as its president for several years—helping to shape nature interpretation throughout the country.

The underground building and entrance walkway at the Naturealm, 1991

Eventually, commissioners realized that the Naturealm had to be expanded. Naturalists were having more and more contacts with the public; the arboretum and nature trails were a growing attraction. The pressure mounted to build not only a larger building, but one as attractive as the grounds on which it would sit.

A confluence of events finally won the day. First, the Cuyahoga Valley National Recreation Area had become a reality, liberating money that had been slated for buying land. The district passed a needed operations levy, ensuring there would be money for staff and maintenance. At about the same time, Director John Daily and Ken Avery had heard about a new building method called the Terra Dome. It snuggled several rectangular rooms together, and mounded soil over top, the weight borne by four concrete pillars. Even though the energy crisis of the 1970s had abated, park staff wanted the building to serve as an example of natural ways to conserve energy. The Terra Dome fit into the district's new, more-natural philosophy. In 1989, commissioners approved a new building at the Natu-realm (now called the Nature Realm). It opened in December 1991. Irene Seiberling Harrison, F.A. Seiberling's daughter, cut the ribbon.

Key to the new building were exhibits that gave visitors the sensa-tion of walking under a larger-than-life stream. Tadpoles the size of large dogs stared out from the transparent tunnel, with water plants and other creatures of the underwater world populating this walk-through exhibit. Stylized leaves hung suspended from the ceiling. The accessible building had an auditorium and classrooms and a sitting area that allowed people to watch birds and other wildlife. Indeed, features like the wildlife window highlighted the Naturealm's role as a place of peace. Its lobby also became the showplace for the last of twenty-four thousand board feet of wormy chestnut that the district purchased in 1951, during the American chestnut blight, and stored at Virginia Kendall. Some concessions were made to the new building. The animal and bee exhibits were removed. The windmill was dismantled and stored in the pre-Civil War barn at Silver Creek Metro Park. The number of naturalists grew from two to four—Szabo retired the year the new visitors center opened—and Walter Starcher took his place.

As modern as the exhibits seemed at the time, most proved static and boring. Within months of the building's grand opening, one exhibit was removed. Another computerized display had to be repaired. The animal exhibits, which children were encouraged to touch, showed wear. By 1998, the exhibits had to be replaced, and the walkway into the visitors center replaced and lighted. This time, the building's design proved a problem. The entrance sat so low, its new sidewalk funneled rainwater into the lobby. It needed to be reworked, again. And the building's natu-ral design was an invitation for woodchucks to burrow into the hillside covering the building.

More important, the busy department had again outgrown its space. Displays had not kept pace with the speed with which understanding of the environment and the natural world had grown. Change was due. The building closed in December 2008 and reopened in March 2010.

The Terra Dome gave physical form to a change in operating philosophy that had begun much earlier. In the late 1980s, commissioners began receiving letters from park users objecting to the pesticides and herbicides the district routinely used to control weeds and insects. The use of herbicides was nothing new to the park district. After persistent leaking at the Gorge ice-skating pond, Harold Wagner determined earthworms were the culprits and ordered caretakers to use chlordane, a potent pesticide and known cancer-causing chemical, to kill the invertebrates.

In addition to pest management, commissioners regularly hired private companies to fertilize lawns and trees. This regimen had begun in the 1970s, before the potential harm was known. As public stewards, they sought to use the best available technology to trim the amount of time that staff put into routine maintenance, freeing them for more intensive work.

Once the public began to react negatively, there was no hesitation to reassess the position. In 1989, commissioners ordered all use of chemicals ended. Park district staff began to use white amur fish to control algae in ponds. They did make some concessions to reality; they continued for a time to use some sprays to repel mice, rats, raccoons and deer, and the district continued to fertilize lawns. In 1993, after finding weeds were winning against maintenance staff's best efforts, the use of Roundup around parking lot posts and signs was again allowed.

Still, a corner had been turned in how commissioners and staff looked at the Metro Parks. Always protective of their literal turf, they also began to broaden their perspective on their role as public stewards. Not only were they protecting the parks' physical space, they were protecting what lived within that space. They began to understand that the parks were ecosystems and needed to be treated as a whole, not seen as a set of singular problems in search of isolated solutions.

The Twinsburg Ledges Area in Liberty Park provides refuge for a variety of species, including endangered Indiana bats.

The search began for best practices, how to provide attractive areas without excessive—if any—use of harmful chemicals. That change in thinking also opened a new vista. If the role of the park district was to connect people with the parks and to protect the wildlife within those parks, it might be a good idea to know what lived within and near the twelve parks the district owned and operated at that time.

In 1999, commissioners added the position of resource management specialist. It eventually became its own department. Rebecca Finder Porath, from Missouri, was the first person to have a close look at the park district's natural resources. In 2002, Mike Johnson, an employee of Davey Tree and a consultant on resource issues, took Porath's place.

Since then, the resource management staff has been charting the natural and archaeological resources within each park and conservation area. That includes plants and animals, geology, rare and invasive species. These natural resource inventories enable staff to plan better and best manage the areas.

The resource management department discovered that the ledges in Liberty Park in Twinsburg were an important hibernation site for endangered Indiana bats and a refuge for a variety of native birds, thus earning the area designation as an Important Bird Area from the Audubon Society. Through the park district's work to preserve the ledges and restore Pond Brook, which runs through Liberty Park, Twinsburg Township—the last remaining holdout from the park district's creation in 1921—and the adjoining community of Reminderville petitioned Probate Court to join the district.

Some resource management isn't fun. The white-tailed deer population in Ohio, once so thin that park officials begged for a statewide moratorium on hunting in the early part of the twentieth century, had more than rebounded. Deer were foraging throughout the Cuyahoga Valley, eating so much of the flora in the parks that entire ecosystems, and the habitat they provide, were threatened. After much discussion, study and public debate—including an unsuccessful lawsuit against the park district's policy—commissioners approved a plan to selectively thin the deer in certain parks each year, with meat from the dressed deer donated to the Akron-Canton Regional Foodbank.

Once the commissioners decided to rethink the way the parks were managed, the course toward environmental stewardship was set. There was new emphasis on conserving the land and what lived in it. Soon that grew to include everything the park district touched. Building audits sought out energy leaks. Some trucks were converted to biodiesel fuel. Restrooms sprouted signs urging users to turn off the lights when the rooms were empty. Paper recycling bins sprouted like wildflowers in parking lots.

The efforts won the district recognition in 1997 from the Army Corps of Engineers as a Conservation and Protection Organization, qualifying it

Restoration work in Liberty Park added meanders to the formerly channelized ditch that was Pond Brook.

to receive money from developers who would be damaging wetlands during development projects in order to restore other wetlands within the same watershed.

One need only look at today's Pond Brook to see the value of such recognition. Once a farm ditch that drained wetlands, the district used funds from the widening and rerouting of State Route 8, north of State Route 303, to turn that stagnant, lifeless ditch back into the meandering creek it had been before farmers tamed the land. Working with Oxbow River & Stream Restoration of Delaware, the ditch was carved, filled with rock and gravel and planted with various native trees and other wetland plants. The results have been worth it. Not only is the nearby wetland coming back to life, but the brook is already increasing in fish and insect populations that had lost the cool, oxygen-rich environment they need to thrive.

With successful conservation projects completed and more in the works, it seems only appropriate that the resource management staff should get its own "green house."

Starting with a 1950s-era brick ranch on Sand Run Parkway the district acquired from the Angelo Cirello family, the district set about to transform it into a LEED (Leadership in Energy and Environmental Design)-certified headquarters for the resource management department and park rangers in the mid-2000s. That meant recycling about 96 percent of items from the house that no longer served a purpose for the parks. Much of those items went to Habitat for Humanity. Some of the material, such as cherry wood flooring, was reworked and used to support counters made

The LEED-certified headquarters for rangers and biologists in Sand Run Metro Park, August 2009

from recycled newspapers. Lockers in the building are made from recycled milk jugs. The carpeting is made from recycled carpet.

Low-flow sinks and composting toilets minimize water use. Geothermal heating lessens the burden on the furnace. Solar arrays generate electricity. Recycled steel roofs funnel water onto a rooftop garden, a rain garden and into rain barrels. A porous brick parking lot allows storm water to filter slowly into the ground instead of into storm sewers.

Neither cheap nor easy, the project won one of Ohio's first platinum LEED certifications from the U.S. Green Building Council, coming in slightly under $1 million. What can't be priced is how much the staff has learned about building, maintaining and "living" in such a house. One

STEPS IN TIME

The visitors center entrance at the Nature Realm, following renovations in 2009 and 2010

of the first places that knowledge went was into the 2009–10 renovation of the visitors center at F.A. Seiberling Nature Realm, which also earned its own platinum LEED designation.

The wormy chestnut from the lobby area was recycled throughout the underground building. Runoff now goes into a new wetland area so that it soaks into the ground and filters back to the water table, instead of being channeled into Sand Run's beleaguered storm sewer system. The new, covered Seneca Deck allows classrooms to remain outside even in bad weather. The lobby, complete with a front desk that mimics a fallen tree trunk, features revolving seasonal themes, tying the inside to the outside. The ever-popular wildlife window remains. The pond exhibit, which for years funneled people through the building, still tells a story but doesn't

82

occupy as much of the building. Naturalist offices have moved from windowless rooms inside the building into its former garage, now fitted with a wall of windows. There also is a Naturalist on Duty desk near the entrance, so trained interpreters can answer visitor questions and point out items of interest—both inside and outside.

As with anything involving the natural world, change is constant. Many of the ornamental trees in the Nature Realm's arboretum, planted in the 1960s as living memorials, had lived beyond their life span and were struggling to stay alive. A memorial wall now holds the names of those who contributed so much to the park district.

Since the Nature Realm reopened to the public in spring 2010, visitors are setting attendance records. At once new and familiar, the Terra Dome and its many gardens and trails have gained new life fulfilling their original mission as examples of how humans can learn to live lightly on the Earth.

CHAPTER SIX

Peace in the Valley

H**UMANS ARE** a funny lot. When there is open space, they feel a need to fill it. Then, when things get too crowded, they rediscover a craving for open space. Nothing shows that more than the fate of the Cuyahoga Valley.

In the 1920s, when the Olmsted Brothers came to this area to help the newly formed Akron Metropolitan Park District literally map out a strategy, the Cuyahoga River Valley captivated them. The broad valley, carved over millennia by glaciers and water, had for generations been a farmed patchwork quilt of forest and open land. They could see the value of keeping this area undeveloped except for farms, but saw no good way to prevent development other than to set land aside using a cumbersome and relatively weak system of scenic easements. This was the Roaring Twenties. Akron had just more than tripled its population. There simply was no easy way to take so much land off the tax duplicate. They focused instead on saving key pieces of this valley: Sand Run, the Ritchie Ledges (where Virginia Kendall State Park eventually took root), the Gorge and several areas abutting the valley. For several decades, that had nearly the same effect as saving the entire valley.

However, at the end of World War II, the postwar baby boom pushed people out of cities in search of their piece of the American dream. That population shift in the early 1950s began to eat at the edges of this geological landmark. The Ohio Turnpike was the opening salvo in what would become a continuing battle between public open space and highway development.

Although the park board was against giving up any of its holdings, Director-Secretary Harold Wagner told the board in 1951 that he believed the proposal by the turnpike commission to take a small, four-acre sliver from the northwest portion of Furnace Run Park was "just about as fortunate as it could possibly be with relation to this Metropolitan Park."

The board members were sanguine about the future; they had already watched the Cleveland Metroparks deal with the turnpike builders. Commissioners would not even talk about payment for damage to the park until the toll road was built and the true extent of the damage known. As part of President Eisenhower's interstate highway movement, the turnpike had set other forces in motion. Property owners in Richfield Township began pressing for rezoning of Ohio 21 to capitalize on its commercial value. The walls were closing in.

Rather than oppose this "radical," move, as Wagner saw it, the board remained neutral on the rezoning but alerted township officials that heavy commercial development would inevitably pollute Furnace Run and Brushwood Lake. Township trustees rejected that proposed rezoning because of opposition from nearby homeowners, but the lull was only temporary. By 1955, the area was rezoned to the edge of the beech woods,

Swimming at Brushwood Lake in Furnace Run Metropolitan Park, July 1949

east of Ohio 21, one of the prizes of the former Brush estate. However, it caused another, far greater problem.

When the turnpike took those four out-of-the-way acres, a remarried Dorothy Brush Walmsley invoked the reversion clause in the 1929 Furnace Run purchase agreement that gave her right to the land, because it was being used for something other than a park. Everyone knew she didn't really want her land back; she wanted money. An eventual out-of-court settlement gave her the payment that the park board would have received from the turnpike commission.

Over the next several years, that court settlement served as the foundation for settlements with the former Mrs. Brush and her daughter over land appropriated not only for the turnpike, but for the relocation of Ohio 21 and construction of Interstate 77, all of which converged on hapless Furnace Run Metropolitan Park. After several legal skirmishes with the board, she eventually sold the remaining 150 acres she still owned near

Each April, an estimated 40,000 daffodils bloom along Furnace Run Metro Park's H.S. Wagner Daffodil Trail, named for the district's first director-secretary. He planted the first bulbs there in the late 1930s.

Furnace Run to the park district—about thirty-five of those to daffodil-loving Harold Wagner—in exchange for getting rid of those reversionary clauses. However, she insisted that the rock placed in memory of her late husband remain.

The issue went far beyond clauses, contracts and money involving one particular piece of land. It was clear, not only to Wagner but to the leaders of park districts throughout the United States, that public parks were the bulls-eye in the highway construction target. Nowhere else were there such large tracts of undeveloped land with a public entity as sole owner. To highway planners, parks were the path of least resistance. While the directors could see the reasoning behind the public works land grab, they also began to push back, knowing that without an organized response, their holdings would be crisscrossed by pavement, and they would abdicate their missions as stewards of open space. In 1961, the heads of Ohio's metropolitan parks formed the Conference of Ohio Park District Executives specifically in response to encroachment of federal highways.

The damage from development showed up quickly in Furnace Run. Silt began to clog Brushwood Lake so fast that by 1956 it was no longer fit for swimming. Development in southern Cuyahoga County was going ahead despite lack of sewer service, threatening Furnace Run, a major tributary of the Cuyahoga River. It appeared inevitable that the area between Cleveland and Akron would develop into one long urban corridor. If the parks did nothing, they would become victims, not stewards of the open space they were created to preserve. As early as 1957, Cleveland Metroparks proposed buying land south of the Cuyahoga County line along the Cuyahoga River as a start to putting the valley into public hands and to forestall, if not avoid completely, that development. That park board did eventually buy the defunct Jaite Paper Mill site along Riverview Road. Still, the deans of Ohio's metropolitan parks—William Stinchcomb and Harold Wagner—were retiring after decades-long tenures. Although longtime Wagner lieutenant Forrest Coup took over, changes in leadership slowed plans for a valley rescue. Fortunately for Summit County, Wagner's retirement coincided with the appointment of real estate expert Forrest Myers as park commissioner. Myers believed he had no higher purpose as a commissioner than to buy land.

The board began to pursue its own strategy of preserving the valley and its historic landmarks, beginning with the Ohio & Erie Canal. The state of Ohio still owned the former transportation route despite the canal corridor's destruction in the Good Friday flood of 1913. Ohio first deeded canal lands north of Route 303 to the park district in 1961, following a year later with land known as the state quarry adjacent to what would become Deep Lock Quarry Metro Park. Eventually, Ohio either sold off or ignored most of its canal properties in Summit County. While some of it went to the cities of Akron or Barberton and some stayed within the control of the Ohio Department of Natural Resources, a large chunk of it went to private owners, causing headaches decades later.

Even as there was a changing of the guard in Northeast Ohio's parks, things were also changing in Washington. Interstate highway construction led by President Eisenhower had raised a massive cry throughout the country over disappearing open space. Presidents Kennedy and then Johnson responded by offering federal money to buy land outside of urban areas through the federal Housing and Home Finance Administration, the forerunner to the Department of Housing and Urban Development. At the same time, area residents were beginning to mobilize against the threat to their beloved Cuyahoga Valley.

The Peninsula Valley Heritage Association formed in 1964, first to save the town's iconic Bronson Memorial Church and later to lobby to preserve the Cuyahoga Valley. One of its founding members was John F. Seiberling, grandson of F.A. Seiberling, who had given Summit County

Congressman John Seiberling. *Courtesy of Stan Hywet Hall & Gardens*

such a magnificent start to its metropolitan park system. As a member of the Tri-County Regional Planning Commission, a quasi-governmental coordinating agency that reviewed applications for federal open-space grants, John F. Seiberling took on the mission to save the valley with personal and professional zeal. His family connection to the land had been generations in the making. He grew up at Stan Hywet, the Seiberling family estate, and some of his fondest memories were of hiking, riding horses and spending time in the region's historic river valley just steps outside his family's back door.

Seiberling knew his vision for the valley had to encompass more than the portion near Akron, and he began working with officials in both the Cuyahoga and Summit county park districts to begin buying available land. In this effort as in so many others, the Seiberlings rarely thought small. The grandson of F.A. Seiberling had in mind a national park the length of the Cuyahoga Valley.

It would be a tough sell. When Hayward Kendall died in 1929, he had left his beloved Virginia Kendall to the federal government, which all but sniffed with disdain that this stretch of historic valley could not possibly meet national park standards. It was no Yellowstone or Yosemite, the poster children for what was worthy of federal protection. In the 1930s, perhaps, it seemed that land would forever be available.

When the federal government rejected the Kendall land, the state stepped in to take on the Ritchie Ledges area, turning it over in 1933 for the Akron Metropolitan Park District. For three decades, Virginia Kendall State Park served the region's scenic and recreational needs well. It also became the biggest and one of the most important focal points in the real estate jigsaw puzzle in the Cuyahoga Valley. As parcels abutting the 1,500-acre reservation became available, the park board bought them.

Not everyone understood or accepted what they were doing. The board had a hard time passing levies in the '60s, because Akron officials and taxpayers saw the district buying land, not developing what it already had. When the board went to the Akron Chamber of Commerce for approval of its 1962 levy, the taxation and legislation committee refused to endorse it because of the board's thirst for new land.

No matter. Under the brief tenure of Director-Secretary Arthur Wilcox and relentlessly prodded before, during and afterward by Forrest Myers, the board developed a comprehensive land-acquisition plan, not just for the valley but for the entire county.

"The boundaries of the Cuyahoga Valley [National Park] are ones we established," recalled Kenneth Avery, the district's landscape architect and, with Director-Secretary John Daily, a moving force in preserving the valley. "I remember when we started. We would drive up every driveway and alley to determine what we could do," he said. He recalled a time when Daily heard of a development in the planning stages for land just south of Virginia Kendall. The board bought an isolated but key piece of land, which halted the developers' plans.

Still, the valley had to vie for scarce dollars and competing pressures. In the early 1960s, the board also bought the Harter Dairy Farm, where southern Summit County touches both Medina and Wayne counties, forming the core of Silver Creek Metro Park. And E. Reginald and Rhea Adam gave the board their beloved Top O' the World Farm in Northampton Township, a key holding on the valley's east rim.

The timing of the Adams' donation gave the park board a chance to gain the land it needed to create Hampton Hills Metro Park without securing any additional funding. The park board swapped land in Goodyear Heights Metro Park for land owned by the city of Akron along Akron-Peninsula Road in Northampton Township—land that once had been used as a garden for the city workhouse.

The Harter Barn in Silver Creek Metro Park, October 1969

The state of Ohio was also getting involved in the effort to save the valley. First, officials reversed the policy of buying only the cheapest land in the state for parks, which effectively limited big parks to the southern part of the state. The Ohio Department of Natural Resources commissioned a recreation study to establish a regional or local park in the valley, with joint management by the Cuyahoga and Summit county park districts. Still, this apparent assistance wouldn't save the valley because ODNR refused to share its federal open-space dollars with local entities. Luckily, state law created metropolitan park districts as legal units of government. They were eligible for federal matching funds on their own.

The urgency only increased. In 1965, with new director John Daily in office barely four months, Ohio Edison announced plans to build high-tension power lines through the middle of the valley, a massive threat to its scenic beauty. At the same time, Ohio Edison's Cuyahoga County

The Adam House at the Top O' the World Farm, now part of Hampton Hills Metro Park

counterpart, the Cleveland Electric Illuminating Co., was planning its own huge power lines traveling south along the river.

Despite protests from both the Cuyahoga and Summit county park districts, the power companies declared their plans a fait accompli. John Seiberling, who attended the park board meeting at which Ohio Edison President Bruce Mansfield affirmed his company's plans to build the lines, redoubled his efforts. By now chairman of the Tri-County Planning Commission, Seiberling sued to stop construction based on the planning group's recently adopted land-use plan calling for preservation of the valley. The Ohio Supreme Court eventually threw out the lawsuit, but the threat of litigation persuaded CEI to hold off building. It would take another fourteen years of litigation to finally end CEI's threat to build power lines through the Cuyahoga Valley.

Highways remained a threat. Despite years of pleading with federal highway planners, the park district lost its appeal to alter the route of

Hughie, Rory and Mrs. O'Neil at the family farm, 1946

Interstate 271 around majestic Brandywine Falls. Construction began in 1968, forever condemning one of the valley's most treasured landscapes to the constant whir and thunder of traffic.

With a strategic plan in hand and as much money as the board could muster from tax revenue, local foundations and the federal government, the buying continued, including more land for Furnace Run and Virginia Kendall. Members began negotiating with General Tire Chairman M. Gerald O'Neil for the family farm that straddled West Bath Road and included an abandoned General Tire Boy Scout camp on the west hillside of the valley. Insurance executive Sherman Schumacher donated a prized piece of land along Cuyahoga Street that he had been quietly acquiring, piece by piece, for years, using it as family picnic grounds. This donation added flesh to the vision, hatched in the mid-1950s, of Sand Run Metro Park stretching from Revere Road to the Gorge.

The 1970 election pushed the preservation of the Cuyahoga Valley into high gear. Seiberling was elected to the U.S. House of Representatives, where he quickly introduced a bill to create a national park in the Cuyahoga Valley. At the same time, newly-elected Ohio Governor John Gilligan's administration included Summit County resident William Nye as head of the Ohio Department of Natural Resources. Nye was so keen

Brandywine Falls is managed by Cuyahoga Valley National Park.

Picnicking at Virginia Kendall Park, August 1939

on preserving the valley that he began to pursue the idea of making it a state park if Seiberling's efforts in Congress failed. The top priority for his department became creating a Cuyahoga Valley park. It eventually became the state's number one federal project. In one of the most dramatic bureaucratic turnarounds, Ohio began to pledge the lion's share of its federal recreation money—about $700,000 a year—to the two park districts' efforts to save the valley.

However, as the Akron Metropolitan Park District was painfully aware, development pressures would not abate. Nick Mileti was building his Coliseum sports and entertainment complex in Richfield Township in 1972. The same year the board watched helplessly as homes began to rise on land it had been seeking for years south of Blossom Music Center. Board minutes are unequivocal: that particular development represented the "first major defeat in the Cuyahoga Valley acquisition plan." Fortunately, the mere turn of a shovel for Towpath Village in Akron so alarmed state officials that Ohio stepped up its land-buying, securing the land slated for the remainder of that subdivision to prevent its expansion onto a crucial eastern valley hillside.

With that purchase, the political tide finally turned. What in the late 1950s had seemed a nearly impossible task—preserving an entire river valley in industrial Northeast Ohio—was close to reality. Echoes of the Olmsted Brothers' misgivings about taking the valley off the tax duplicate rang in stiff opposition to the idea from many valley residents and Peninsula officials. But even the staunchest opponent conceded that life as a small piece in an urban megalopolis would have had far more dire consequences for their peaceful valley than as part of a new national park. Congress passed Seiberling's bill creating the Cuyahoga Valley National Recreation Area in 1974. President Gerald Ford signed it in January 1975.

Fishing at Virginia Kendall Park, September 1976

But the victory for the Cuyahoga Valley required a steep sacrifice for the district that had been its champion for so long. Virginia Kendall State Park, for thirty years the crown jewel among the park district's green islands, was to be turned over to the National Park Service—the same agency that had rejected it so long ago—as part of Ohio's agreement to cede all state land to the federal government when the Cuyahoga Valley National Park was created. With the national park a reality, Virginia Kendall left the park district's care in 1978.

Nonetheless, the idea that had been born in the Akron Metropolitan Park District's boardroom was a reality, and the Seiberling family legacy as protectors of the land and the public good is anchored in the valley's still-forested hillsides.

CHAPTER SEVEN

Long and Winding Trail

While the Cuyahoga and Summit county park districts were in the same business—preserving open space for public use—they began to look very different from the outset. Cleveland Metroparks became the Emerald Necklace, with its parks, called reservations, forming a large semicircle south of Lake Erie. Summit County's park district sprouted to include Metro Parks that looked like green islands on a map.

Nonetheless, there was land worth saving that did not come in clumps of acres; it looked more like ribbons. These long, thin strips eventually helped create valuable connections to other important public projects. First, however, they had to be preserved. The case is no clearer than with what was left of the Ohio & Erie Canal.

There is no question this area owes its prosperity to the canal. Still, it is also true that the canal was little more than old folks' memories for

Lock 13, near the Mustill Store, before the flood of 1913

decades, with only a few artifacts, aging houses and canal remnants to speak for it.

By the turn of the twentieth century, railroads had already supplanted the canal as the major mode of transportation and commerce. Early in the 1900s, the state tried to revive the waterway for carrying bulk goods, but nature had other plans. A devastating late-March flood in 1913 forced the dynamiting of locks the length of the canal to save the cities that had grown up along its route. There were half-hearted efforts to save what remained. The conversations that eventually led to the creation of the Akron Metropolitan Park District were spurred by a proposal from Alling DeForest, commissioned by Harvey Firestone, for a study of possible parks in Akron. That report urged Akron to work with the new Cuyahoga County park board to secure the canal lands that ran between the two cities and create a road to link them. It is arguable that without the effort to save the canal, the Akron Metropolitan Park District might never have

The flood of 1913 destroyed parts of Akron and officially ended the canal era.

Spectators watch an Akron house being swept away in the 1913 flood.

been formed because there was no entity in Summit County capable of taking on that kind of project. But that, as they say, is history.

More to the point, the Olmsted Brothers advocated that the canal itself be preserved for boating, particularly the stretch of canal from Akron through Summit Lake south past Nesmith Lake and into Barberton. Even though many private owners already controlled parts of the canal through the cities, the Olmsteds thought highly enough of the waterway to suggest public agencies buy the immediate banks and other pieces of adjacent real estate that could lend themselves to parks along the way.

That never happened. Other priorities, other pieces of land needed immediate attention. The idea of preserving the canal waned. Akron was a busy city, getting on with its central role in the rubber industry. Except for those industries and homeowners who planted themselves along the remaining pieces of the canal, the waterway disappeared from public consciousness. Akron even buried part of the canal that ran through downtown under skyscrapers that passed as urban renewal.

Lock 28, the deepest lock on the Ohio & Erie Canal, in Deep Lock Quarry Metro Park, 1960s

One small piece of Summit County canal history remained. The quarry that had provided Berea sandstone for so much of the region's nineteenth-century building boom, and much of the growth of the Industrial Revolution throughout the country, nestled by the canal at Lock 28. Given to the park board in 1934, it remained undeveloped until the 1960s. After the state donated its own quarry lands adjacent to Deep Lock and two portions of the towpath trail in 1961 and '62, the park district developed the old quarry and opened Deep Lock Quarry Metro Park in 1964. It included part of the towpath, the trail along which mule teams pulled canal boats, which did not have their own power. That remnant ran from the park south to Everett Road.

There was not much traffic along this historic pathway. "No one could ride on it because there were trees growing in the towpath," recalled Ken Avery, the park district's former landscape architect, in 2009.

It remained little more than potential until the National Park Service established the Cuyahoga Valley National Recreation Area. One of the first projects after the park finished acquiring land was reconstructing nearly twenty miles of the Towpath Trail through the valley between Akron and the Cuyahoga County line. At the same time, a group of Akron preservationists persuaded the city to buy the dilapidated but historic Mustill Store and locktender's house at Lock 15. That group eventually became Cascade Locks Park Association in 1989. In 1996, Congress created the Ohio & Erie Canal National Heritage Corridor, designating a sliver of land running between Lake Erie and Dover along the canal route worthy of preservation and pledging federal assistance to save it.

That kind of momentum got Akron officials to rethink how it would repave and widen Riverview Road from the city limits north to accommodate bicyclists. Instead, planners wondered whether an off-road bike trail extending the towpath into Akron might be a better use of resources.

But the keystone to this historic and geographic puzzle actually had been put in place in 1975, when Akron and the park district board joined forces to create and manage Cascade Valley Park along Cuyahoga Street. Little short of a miracle, that agreement became the fulcrum on which the much later Towpath Trail would be leveraged.

The strained relationship between Akron and the metropolitan park board was no secret; it had existed nearly from the district's creation. As the district bought and developed land in Akron, and as the city improved streets near those parks, the city levied assessments on the park board. Commissioners objected because, they reasoned, the parks were public entities and derived no benefit from those improvements. That stalemate—assessment and objection—froze relationships for decades. Tensions only grew in the early 1960s after the city tunneled under the Continental Divide on North Hawkins Avenue. The purpose was to relieve flooding in the new homes that were being built in West Akron. But that storm runoff, which naturally would have flowed south toward the Ohio River watershed, instead flowed north into Sand Run Metro Park, causing erosion so damaging that the parkway was routinely undermined.

What changed was an agreement between the city and the park district to operate a park in what had been a city landfill. The landfill opened in 1958 on property on the east side of Cuyahoga Street that the board had bought at the start of the Great Depression. Nothing had been done to the property, other than allowing inmates from the city workhouse space to raise vegetables. Another city landfill had been operating west of Cuyahoga Street on the site of the old sewer treatment plant, but it had been filled and closed. The park board agreed to allow the city to use the Yule property as a landfill for ten years.

By the mid-1970s, the newer landfill had closed. Even though the land belonged to the park board, the city had agreed to maintain it. That maintenance proved to be a problem.

"I remember driving through the ooze that ran onto Cuyahoga Street from the landfill," said Bert Szabo. Trash was eroding into the river, and methane gas was building. In 1975, city officials suggested the park board join in a partnership in which the city would redevelop the old landfill into ball fields and parking lots if the park district would maintain and operate them. Commissioners were wary because of their history with the city. They worried about this agreement's impact on future levies. And they feared second-guessing by Akron City Council.

But the moment seemed right. The city was interested in the Mustill Store and locktender's house near the southern end of Cuyahoga Street, suggesting the tantalizing possibility of a canal-themed park running from downtown Akron to Cascade Valley and including the nearby towpath. The confluence of events lent a sense of logic to a Cascade Valley Park. The master plan for Cascade Valley, including the future Cascade Locks area, was completed in 1979. Eventually, Cascade Locks Park would develop as an independent area.

The Mustill Store catered to Akron residents and travellers on the Ohio & Erie Canal.

By the 1980s, the boarded-up Mustill Store was an eyesore and it was almost razed.

That historic agreement didn't end the tussle between the city and the park district. Park officials, especially maintenance chief John Kasarda, a stickler schooled in the Forrest Coup school of meticulous maintenance, did not think the quality of the work done by the city was good enough for the park system, calling into question such details as using broken cement as riprap along the curves of the Cuyahoga River. Eventually, the park district agreed to design the park with the city reimbursing expenses. Finally,

Today, the Mustill Store is home to the Cascade Locks Park Association and includes displays explaining the area's importance to the canal and the development of Akron.

the Oxbow section of Cascade Valley Park, appropriately named for its signature bend in the Cuyahoga, opened in 1982. Later, when the city finished buying the remaining houses on Peck Road and turned that land into the Chuckery Area, plans for soccer fields along the river could proceed. That purchase also protected a wetland near Cuyahoga Street and finally gave naturalists access to a massive burr oak near the river, which residents of this area have long called the Signal Tree. It is thought that natives using the historic Portage Path looked for this tree as a sign they were near the spot where they would take their canoes out of the Cuyahoga and portage south to the Tuscarawas River.

It is hard to overstate the importance of that first partnership. Once officials had experience working together, they could move beyond the strained past. Certainly, there would continue to be frictions on other issues, most notably storm water erosion in Sand Run Metro Park. But friction was no longer a barrier. As retired city planner Tom Long pointed out, decades later when the city began to develop its canal resources in

The Signal Tree in Cascade Valley's Chuckery Area

earnest, the park district did not need to have its arm twisted to join in. Once the towpath from Botzum south was complete, the park district took over maintenance, a template that has smoothed development of the Towpath Trail. As other Summit County organizations began to see benefits to developing their pieces of the canal, and the larger benefits of partnerships, they sought the park district's help.

The park district's involvement persuaded PPG Industries to open its section of towpath in 2003. Director-secretary Keith Shy and PPG Industries' senior remediation engineer Bill Lynch shared many interests, and that relationship turned the corporation from wariness about the towpath to enthusiasm. There were tricky environmental issues involved in this small, three-quarter-mile section of the towpath, which passed near the company's lime lakes. That area had been the company's caustic chemicals dump, barren of vegetation and wildlife. The company was already cleaning up that site, but it did not want to take on more liability or expense. Shy used the park district's experience to allay PPG's concerns.

At the end of 2010, the park district managed 21.5 miles of towpath in Akron and reaching south to the border of Stark County. That year, an agreement with the Wheeling & Lake Erie Railroad cleared the final barrier to completing the trail though Barberton. The Towpath Trail is scheduled to be complete through Summit County by late 2011.

The Cuyahoga River, as seen from the Overlook Deck in Cascade Valley Metro Park

The towpath is only one of many recreational opportunities opened by defunct transportation lines. While the Olmsteds were partial to parkways and elongated land holdings, even they could not have foreseen the rapid demise of passenger rail service throughout the industrial Northeast. Railroads, having effectively killed the canal system, were supplanted by trucks and cars traveling Eisenhower's national network of highways. In 1968, the park board heard of abandoned rail lines and saw another opportunity to build trails in these land corridors. In 1970, Ohio Edison agreed to lease its tension-line corridor near Portage County for such a trail. Combined with the old interurban rail line, the first segment of the Bike & Hike Trail was taking shape, becoming one of the country's first rails-to-trails conversions. The first fifteen miles, developed beginning in 1971, stretched from the Portage County line through Munroe Falls

Congressman John Seiberling speaks at the dedication of the Bike & Hike Trail, 1972

and Stow, skirting Hudson and bending toward Cuyahoga County. Was it only coincidence that, as the park district's influence reached northward, Hudson would finally ask to be included in the taxing district? The annexation was complete in 1972. The first six miles of crushed-limestone trail opened in April 1973. Sixteen miles were complete by 1976.

Developing the Bike & Hike Trail created pressure for a park in the northeast section of the county. As early as 1961, Summit County commissioners had suggested the park district buy the land occupied by the Summit County Home, which was to close in 1970. The park board for a time tried to buy land along Fish Creek in Stow after the Cuyahoga Valley National Recreation Area was a reality and district officials had money to buy elsewhere. However, rapid development in that area put land prices out of reach.

In 1977, the board learned that Renner's, the popular swimming park in Munroe Falls, was up for sale. It was clear that the Village of Munroe Falls also wanted to buy the property, but with plans for a Fish Creek park falling apart, Renner's became an attractive alternative to the Akron Metropolitan Park District. In April 1978, the board bought Renner's, for a time kicking up a storm of protest from Munroe Falls. This purchase again enabled the district to offer swimming. The lakes at Virginia Kendall and Furnace Run had closed to swimmers in the late 1950s.

The Bike & Hike Trail continued to grow in length and popularity, its tendrils extending out from its spine. Stow lobbied for a connection with the main trail through Silver Springs Park. By the late 1990s, the trail was twenty-three miles long. It now stretches a total of 33.5 miles, connecting Summit County with the biking trails in the Cleveland Metroparks'

Congressman Seiberling was one of the first to ride on the Bike & Hike Trail.

Brecksville Reservation, echoing the Olmsteds' desire to connect the best of the region's open spaces. Eventually, the entire trail would be paved in asphalt, the crushed limestone proving too vulnerable to erosion.

Trails offered an alternative to gyms for fitness buffs. Philanthropist Ruth Roush approached board members about a combination walking and exercise trail made popular in Europe. Her donation in 1975 created the district's first Parcours Trail in the Treaty Line Area of Sand Run Metro Park. A similar course was later installed in Goodyear Heights Metro Park.

For many people, running was the exercise of choice, putting joggers and cars in competition for space on beautiful Sand Run Parkway. Commissioners decided to give joggers and hikers a trail of their own, building

Year-round, the Jogging Trail in Sand Run Metro Park is easily the district's busiest trail.

a six-foot wide path between Portage Path and Sand Run Road on the north hillside paralleling the parkway. Keith Shy, at the time superintendent of maintenance, was against it.

"Dead set against it," he recalled. "We had to take out so many trees."

Work began in 1987 and finished three years later. Shy, who would become director-secretary in 1998, now embraces the trail as one of the district's biggest successes. On average, more than one thousand people use the jogging trail every day year-round. It has been so successful that the Jogging Trail was extended beyond Sand Run Road to Revere Road in 2006.

It is now possible for a hiker or jogger to travel on foot from Revere Road, through Sand Run Metro Park, over to the Big Bend Area off Merriman Road, along the Towpath Trail, eventually winding up in the gravel parking lot at the Schumacher Area of Cascade Valley on Cuyahoga Street, all on land owned or maintained by Metro Parks. Another long-held dream come true.

CHAPTER EIGHT

Making Friends

I**N THE WORLD OF METROPOLITAN PARK SYSTEMS,** it takes friends to prosper. That means people who use the parks. On that score, the Summit County park system is wealthy. Visitation topped five million in 2010.

It also takes friends to get things done that otherwise would have to be done by staff. In that regard, early park officials found valuable relationships with both the Girl Scouts and the Izaak Walton League.

During the Depression, Girl Scouts attended Happy Days Camp at Virginia Kendall, both as a daytime campsite and for overnight camping. In return, they stepped in to fill staff shortages caused by World War II, helping with enrollment for the camp when city workers were too busy tending their own playgrounds. They later used both Virginia Kendall and Firestone for day camps for Summit County scout troops. In time, scout camps would expand to most of the parks' shelters.

Girl Scouts plant trees at Goodyear Heights Metropolitan Park, 1933

More than growing memories, the scouts left behind a permanent legacy. Nearly every park in the system is alive with trees. Girl Scouts planted thousands of them. The practice started with Wagner, who never kept track of how many trees the scouts planted—Boy Scouts did some planting, too—but by the mid-1980s, records suggest Girl Scouts in Summit County had planted more than 8,100 trees in the various Metro Parks. Mostly they planted white pines, tulip poplars, oaks and maples.

A reporter for the *Akron Beacon Journal* hiked in 2008 with a group of former scouts who, forty years earlier, had been part of planting five thousand white oak, black walnut and green ash trees at Top O' the World, part of Hampton Hills Metro Park. The scouts had grown from girls to women, and those seedlings now towered over them. Their work reminded them of the scouts' principle of leaving the world better than they found it.

Boy Scouts have also left their mark, volunteering for events and contributing countless Eagle Scout projects, like footbridges and help with hiking trails.

Girl Scouts plant trees on Arbor Day at
O'Neil Woods Metropolitan Park, 1974

Children who have fished the waters in the Metro Parks have the Izaak Walton League to thank. Beginning in the 1950s, as Virginia Kendall Lake closed to swimming, it opened to fishing. With support from the League, Metro Parks staff would stock the lakes with game fish. Part of the incentive was trying to catch fish that League members had tagged. In the first several years, anglers earned 50 cents per tagged fish. Later, the prize grew to a silver dollar. Programs continued at Virginia Kendall and later moved to Firestone.

Today, an annual trout derby at Little Turtle Pond in Firestone Metro Park is co-sponsored by the Goodyear Hunting & Fishing Club and the Ohio Department of Natural Resources, Division of Wildlife.

The greatest need for friends comes at levy time. The parks operate on money raised from a countywide property tax levy. In the district's first years, it did not operate on its own tax revenue but on what was shared

Gertrude Seiberling. *Courtesy of Stan Hywet Hall & Gardens*

from the county's general fund. As the district grew, it became clear that the parks would need their own dedicated source of income.

At first, campaigns were run in-house. In the 1920s and '30s, there was no prohibition against park employees engaging in political campaigning. For the first levy in 1928, Wagner joined women from the Akron Garden Club—of which Gertrude Seiberling was a prominent member—to campaign for the passage of a .10-mill levy, which raised about $50,000. That levy passed, as did a second ten years later. However, in 1939, Congress passed the Hatch Act, which bars government employees from direct political activity. Clearly, front-office levy efforts would have to change.

For several campaigns, the appointed commissioners ran the levies, either taking care of publicity or handling the money raised by people who did not work for or run the district. Commissioner Mark Kindig ran the first post-Hatch Act levy in 1947. Later, he worked with community leader Bert Polsky and a "Committee of 100," which promoted all levies in Summit County. However, their ace in the hole remained Wagner, who was a one-man public-relations machine. If he wasn't guiding nature hikes or broadcasting programs on the radio, he was in the parks or schools, always selling his message of the benefits of the outdoors.

That kind of effort had its limits. By the mid-1950s, Wagner was ready to retire. Voters did not understand the difference between the countywide Akron Metropolitan Park District and Akron city parks. Complaints about city parks were blamed on the AMPD. For whatever reason, levies began to fail regularly. The board hired a public relations consultant in March 1958, but Robert Hollister quit six months later

Boy Scouts pose with shovels
at the Gorge, 1963

Boy Scouts serve hot dogs at the
Pops 'N More concert in Firestone
Metro Park, 2010

because the "prevailing attitude of indecision and lack of organization makes it impossible for us to assist the board in accomplishing its public relations goals or developing any concrete plans." Another failed levy in 1958 left the parks dangerously close to closing.

The first in-house public relations staff member came on board in 1959. Matt Hall's title put him in charge of safety and education. He also began to coordinate the 1959 levy. However, the district was accused of giving Hall public money for political gain. He resigned his public job and began raising private contributions to run the campaign. This time the levy passed. Hall rejoined the staff. The parks stayed open.

It went this way for several years, Hall running campaigns part time out of a private office, hiring his own staff to avoid Hatch Act entanglements.

Community volunteers did the legwork and raised the money. However, by the late 1960s and early 1970s, the early environmental movement was taking root. Interest in the Metro Parks and in open space was rising. The Cuyahoga and Summit county park districts were feverishly buying land for the Cuyahoga Valley, holding public meetings with officials and area residents. There was interest in helping the parks independent of levy campaigns. As early as 1971, Akron industrial designer F. Eugene Smith and others calling themselves Friends of the Parks were meeting in Smith's house, looking for ways to help. Commissioners rebuffed their overtures.

As the district was getting flak about its hunger for land from the Akron Regional Development Board, it considered appointing a citizens advisory committee to study the development board's recommendations. Instead, staff took on that job. In 1976, the idea of a Friends group gained greater traction during another levy campaign. Both the League of Women Voters and the Junior League endorsed the idea of some sort of permanent friends group. People calling themselves Friends of the Metropolitan Parks continued to meet, even drawing up preliminary by-laws. Still, in 1977, commissioners formally rejected the idea of a Friends group. The lack of a permanent Friends group devolved into "a group of dedicated people who got together to work feverishly on levy campaigns in 1986 and 1990."

Identity began to factor into levy campaigns, and in the mid-1980s park commissioners asked for help from the University of Akron's survey research experts to gauge community support for and understanding of the parks. However, it continued to stonewall a formal group of supporters.

This standoffishness hurt the park district. As it prepared for its 1986 levy campaign, community leaders John Feudner and Eddie Butler approached many of the people who had helped in the past. Because the board had not followed through on requests to formally recognize a Friends group, Feudner and Butler were hard-pressed to find willing helpers. Yet they did, and the levy passed.

In 1987, commissioners William Zekan, Robert Mercer and William Blodgett changed the public identity of the district to Metro Parks, Serving Summit County, although the ballot would continue to say Akron Metropolitan Park District until it was legally changed through Probate Court in 1995. A logo competition among University of Akron art students introduced the iconic maple leaf, and the commissioners bought into a formal publicity program.

Finally, in 1990, facing strained relationships with Akron over long-standing issues of unpaid assessments, park officials were told by their longtime levy volunteers that the price of volunteer help for that year's levy would be creation of a Friends group. The pressure worked; Friends of Metro Parks formed in January 1991 and the group was officially announced just before Earth Day that year.

There was no shortage of issues for the Friends to tackle, and their influence was felt from the outset. During the 1990 levy campaign, Akron Mayor Don Plusquellic had broached the idea that the Metro Parks consider taking over the Akron Zoological Park, just as Cleveland Metroparks had taken on the Cleveland Zoo in 1970.

"I think the city was trying to unload the zoo," recalled Robert Freitag, first president of Friends of Metro Parks. "They wanted us [Metro Parks] to take it on." As part of the zoo package, the city also suggested the park take over the Ed Davis Community Center in nearby Perkins Park, sparking controversy because Ed Davis opposed the idea. Park commissioners, staff and the larger community, including the editorial page of the *Akron Beacon Journal*, seemed inclined toward taking it on. Freitag polled members of Friends, three-fourths of whom were against the idea.

"We had a meeting at Firestone," Freitag said. "Everyone was on board but the Friends." Freitag dug a bit further into the issue, visiting

Cleveland Metroparks director Vern Hartenberg and one of Cleveland's park commissioners about their experience running a zoo. He asked bluntly how the Clevelanders felt.

"They advised us not to do it," Freitag said. Akron officials eventually went a different direction, putting a successful levy for the zoo on the ballot in March 2000.

The creation of Friends began to result in different kinds of programs. The group helped begin the Fall Family Outing, featuring campfires, stories and hayrides at Goodyear Heights Metro Park.

"We thought that about three hundred people would show up," recalled Vivian Harig, third president of Friends of Metro Parks and daughter of former park commissioner Forrest Myers. "Three thousand showed up."

In 1991, almost at the same time Friends was organizing, commissioners were searching for a solution to dead spots in the rangers' mobile radio service. The transmitters were mounted in Richfield and simply could not reach the entire park system. Commissioners thought they had found a solution in a proposal from General Telephone and Electric to build a cell tower at the Nature Realm. The telephone company offered not only to put the park district's communications transmitters on the tower, but also to build an observation deck for the public.

Commissioners, led by Goodyear CEO Bob Mercer, were set on the idea, even approving the tower despite opposition from Friends and even the staff. Employees were particularly upset because the new visitors center at the Nature Realm had been built underground to preserve the natural setting. In a letter to the board, the staff said: "For over twenty-seven years the park district has been creating an area that attempts to take visitors from their highly developed environment into a natural setting. We even have taken special care to subdue the new visitors center building by constructing it underground. A monopole tower, with or without the observation tower, seems to contradict most of what we have been working toward."

The Fall Family Outings are held the first two Saturdays in October; Goodyear Heights Metro Park plays host to the first, Silver Creek Metro Park hosts the second.

Despite having approved the tower, the stiff opposition made Mercer literally take another look, hiring a bucket truck that lifted him seventy-five feet, about the level of the proposed observation deck, so he could see what the public would see. Freitag was on the ground and a staff member was in the bucket with Mercer, snapping photographs. Mercer wasn't impressed with the view. On his way down, he signaled thumbs down to Freitag. He later told Freitag all he could see was the tops of the trees, certainly not to downtown as had been hoped. The commissioners rescinded the tower proposal.

A tangible artifact came from that bucket truck trip. Staff member Phyllis Boerner took a photograph of the top of the visitors center, and it became a popular postcard sold for years at the Nature Realm. No longer on staff, Boerner remains a member of Friends.

Volunteers lead golf cart tours on the Towpath Trail in Clinton. The program, for residents of Summit County retirement communities, was started in 2010.

Perhaps the most important contribution Friends of Metro Parks made was to provide a channel for the pent-up energy and talent of people who wanted to help. Once fliers for Friends were printed, including space for people to indicate interest, volunteers began to pour in.

In 1995, the park district logged 4,500 hours of volunteer service. Not bad for an organization that only four years earlier had no tradition of volunteerism. A year later a part-time volunteer coordinator was hired, and the position would eventually become a full-time role. By 2011, more than 500 registered volunteers were contributing over 30,000 service hours per year.

The story has an ironic twist. Because Friends is a nonprofit organization, it cannot legally give money directly to the park district. Its role in supporting levy campaigns is limited to volunteering. But that problem was solved in 1993 with the creation of the popular STOMP Bicycle Adventure.

More than twelve hundred riders participate in STOMP every year. The event raises funds for Citizens for Metro Parks.

STOMP has stood for the "September Tour of Metro Parks," the "Summer Tour of Metro Parks" and the "Summit Tour of Metro Parks."

This family oriented bicycling event, which began as a naturalist-led program, now raises money for levies while taking participants through Metro Parks and the Cuyahoga Valley National Park, building yet another bond between people and the park system. It is held the Saturday of Labor Day weekend and organized by Citizens for Metro Parks, a political action committee.

It is hard to imagine the Metro Parks without friends, whether in the form of a formal organization or simply the hundreds of volunteers who annually give their time to about every department in the park district. They catalog natural resources, teach winter camping skills, answer phone calls, ride the multipurpose trails to assist hikers and cyclists, sign hiking spree forms, and more. It is clear that Metro Parks, Serving Summit County has thousands of connections into its community, relationships that benefit not only the park district, but also those who are eager to serve it.

CHAPTER NINE

The Gorge

EACH OF THE METRO PARKS HAS ITS OWN STORY, tied to the farmers, land barons, industrial giants and regular citizens who made their lives in and around them. But few stories are as engaging as the cliff-hangers that have enveloped Gorge Metro Park, which straddles Akron and Cuyahoga Falls.

The Great Falls, or Coppocaw, as it was called by the Indians who camped along its rapids, has long been an awe-inspiring landmark. Its history includes the saga of Mary Campbell, reportedly abducted by the Delaware Indians in 1765, and brought to the shallow cave that now bears her name. It includes the failed industrial fantasy of Dr. Eliakim Crosby, who thought he could duplicate his success of the Cascade Race, which powered mills on the banks of the Ohio & Erie Canal in Akron. He sought to create Summit City at the foot of the Chuckery Race on the

A couple poses in the Gorge, 1890s

south bank of the Cuyahoga River at the Gorge. Only the cut sandstone walls of that failed race remain.

The history includes the boatmen who took tourists on scenic rides to the edge of the rapids from Gaylord's picnic grove for a dime. It includes the kids and families who crowded the north shore, beginning in the late 1800s, to visit a succession of amusement parks where they rode one of the nation's oldest roller coasters, ate chicken from Mrs. Fosdick's tavern above Old Maid's Kitchen (Mary Campbell Cave) or simply strolled along the rock cliffs with such colorful names as Lovers Retreat, Fern Cave, Weeping Cliffs, Dove Cave, the Snake's Den or Goose Egg Island.

It also includes the creation of the 57-feet high, 429-feet wide dam that is now the area's most defining feature, putting its industrial stamp on the rock-hard scenery. Whether that mark is indelible or whether Coppocaw returns remains one of the cliff-hangers.

Mary Campbell Cave was named for a twelve-year-old Pennsylvania girl, reportedly captured in 1759 by the Delaware and brought to the Gorge, becoming the first white child in the wild frontier of the Western Reserve.

Even as park commissioners were negotiating for the donation of the Northern Ohio Traction & Light Company's 144 acres, the forerunner of Ohio Edison was contemplating lease of the area to yet another amusement park. Those plans died in December 1929, when the company announced the donation of the Gorge to the Akron Metropolitan Park District just before Christmas.

If park officials thought the donation and their stewardship would be the end of human interference in the Gorge, they were naïve. Included in the donation was NOTL's reservation of rights to operate a small hydroelectric plant on the south side of the Cuyahoga River. Those structures, used or not, would remain in place until 1958, when Ohio Edison abandoned the facility and dismantled most of the machinery.

The Great Falls, or Coppocaw, 1890s

For a time, the Gorge served as a geologist's laboratory, affording countless University of Akron and Kent State University students a chance to understand how natural forces shaped the scenery, its fossil record serving as a natural timeline for hints of the former inland sea and the river's relentless carving of the landscape. It played host to film crews who found the steep sandstone cliffs hard to resist for dramatic action shots.

But the area was too close to civilization to remain untouched, or at least to stay off planners' drawing boards. Some of those plans made sense. In 1955, the park district spearheaded an effort to create a park from Akron's defunct Highbridge Park and the vacated off-ramp of the old High-Level Bridge, to join the Gorge with what would later become the Chuckery Area of Cascade Valley Park. That idea surfaced at about the same time that Ray Stuliffe of the *Akron Beacon Journal*, Mayor Wolfe of Cuyahoga Falls and C.R. Quine of Akron proposed to restore the deep gorge paralleling Front Street, from the Ohio Edison power plant to the Prospect Street bridge in the Falls. Neither idea gained traction, although a rough outline of the park proposal can be seen in the Highbridge Trail that now links the two park units, making it possible to hike from the Gorge in North Akron nearly to Sand Run Metro Park in West Akron.

Later, state highway planners, grown accustomed to sitting roads through publicly owned land, articulated their vision of a rerouted State Route 8 through the south side of the Gorge. These were the same planners who earlier had suggested placing the same Route 8 through beloved Virginia Kendall State Park. The Akron Metropolitan Park District had already lost several battles with the Ohio Turnpike Commission and federal highway planners, a diminished and damaged Furnace Run as primary evidence. It was not about to let the Gorge experience the same fate. Akron and Cuyahoga Falls officials, joining the adamant and by now savvy park board, successfully kept the Gorge and Virginia Kendall intact. Route 8 shifted slightly south of the park, preserving historic landmarks such as the remnants of the Chuckery Race and the stands of native hemlock that have called the Gorge home for millennia.

Still, it was hard to keep industrial dreams quiet. Former Akron Mayor Roy Ray resurrected the notion of hydroelectric power in the early 1980s with his proposal to rebuild Ohio Edison's abandoned hydro facilities. Ray was looking for a cheaper way to power the city's Botzum sewage treatment plant. He also suggested building a small hydro plant at the city's Lake Rockwell. Ray's plans went nowhere. However, they sowed hardy seeds.

In 1998, a group calling itself Universal Electric Power Corp. proposed testing a new kind of hydroelectric turbine using water cascading over the Gorge dam. At that time, park district officials used that proposal as an opportunity to educate park users about new kinds of energy—or, better, newly rediscovered forms—and worked with Universal to build a walkway opposite the company's experimental plant to interpret the work.

Universal said it was optimistic at being able to provide power for about 100 to 150 homes, but ran afoul of securities laws and closed in 2004, abandoning several projects the company said it had in Ohio and neighboring states.

At about the same time, another company, Advanced Hydro Solutions of Fairlawn, filed a permit application with the Federal Energy Regulatory Commission to study building a hydroelectric plant in the same spot used by Universal, using what appeared to be much the same technology. This time, however, the political and environmental landscape had shifted.

The Ohio Environmental Protection Agency had been conducting a survey of the many dams across Ohio's rivers. The EPA said the science was fairly conclusive: With Clean Water Act regulations calling for greater oxygen levels in the state's rivers, communities along dammed rivers had a choice to either spend millions in public dollars to build state-of-the-art treatment facilities to boost oxygen levels, or take down their dams. Kent and Munroe Falls had already chosen: The Munroe Falls dam was dismantled to its bedrock foundation and Kent's dam was altered to bypass the worst effects.

The next dam downstream from Munroe Falls is the gigantic Ohio Edison dam in the Gorge. Removing it would be neither easy nor cheap. Estimates made in 2004 suggested it would cost about $10 million to remove the Gorge dam. Staggering, but just a part of the cost. Removing sediment that had collected behind it, assumed to contain heavy metals and other toxins, could add at least another $50 million to the tab.

In 2005, Ohio Edison turned over to Metro Hydroelectric Co., a subsidiary of Advanced Hydro Solutions, the easements that NOTL had reserved in 1929 to continue to operate and maintain its hydro plant.

Metro Parks officials had once been open to experimentation. This time, with a more ambitious proposal at hand, they saw what kind of damage the park would sustain from even a feasibility study, which would

The Ohio Edison plant on the Cuyahoga River was demolished in 2009.

include grading steep slopes for a road on the south side of the river and removing trees on four acres. A rare stand of native northern monkshood plants, listed as threatened by the federal government and entitled to federal protection, could have been wiped out. And some of the region's most beautiful scenery would have been forever altered. As stewards of the public trust, park commissioners could not allow such a threat.

A 2005 public hearing into the hydroelectricity proposal attracted a standing-room-only crowd representing an array of governmental, environmental and private groups opposed to Metro Hydroelectric's proposal. It was at that meeting that Cuyahoga Falls Mayor Don Robart dubbed the park district "the environmental conscience of Summit County."

In 2006, park commissioners formally opposed the Metro Hydroelectric project, vowing to "do all things necessary and proper" to fight it. It barred any access by Metro Hydroelectric employees to the park. That

The endangered northern monkshood grows in few places, yet Gorge Metro Park is one of them. Efforts to save the plants are slowly increasing the local population.

The dam still stands, unused to generate hydropower for decades.

hard line was generally supported in the larger community, with such groups as the Ohio Environmental Council, Friends of the Crooked River and the governments of many of the communities that line the Cuyahoga River in Summit County adding their approval.

Advanced Hydro sued in federal court seeking to force Metro Parks to open the Gorge for the study. A series of rulings ensued, eventually barring Metro Hydroelectric from entering the property. In 2007, the FERC terminated Metro Hydroelectric's permit application because it could not gain access for the feasibility study. In September 2008, the Sixth U.S. Circuit Court of Appeals ruled that the battle was not a federal case but a private property issue governed by Ohio law. It dismissed Metro Hydroelectric's lawsuit. In October 2008, Metro Hydroelectric reapplied to the FERC for a permit. However, there was no action on that reapplication, and it expired March 31, 2009.

Ohio Edison removed the long-dormant Gorge power plant from the west riverbank in 2009, but the issue of removing the dam has not evaporated. In September 2009, the U.S. Environmental Protection Agency

An aerial view of the dam in the Gorge

sampled the riverbed behind the dam to determine the kinds of toxic material that has accumulated since 1910.

Preliminary results did not show serious toxic contamination, as was feared. Still, the sludge was deemed toxic enough that it would have to be removed before the dam could come down. Preliminary estimates suggest 500,000 cubic yards of polluted muck are piled at the bottom of the dam.

Who will pay to have it removed? Will the dam fall? Yet more cliff-hangers for the Gorge.

CHAPTER TEN

Further Steps

AN ORGANIZATION RICH IN HISTORY—both human and natural—Metro Parks, Serving Summit County is also a living entity, infused with the energy of the people who work in, volunteer for and visit its many parks, trails and attractions. And it continues to grow.

Springfield Township residents are enjoying one of the newest additions, Springfield Bog Metro Park, which opened January 5, 2011 off Portage Line Road. For several years, the park district worked with the Trust for Public Land, a private nonprofit that often buys important pieces of land and turns them over to public agencies, to acquire the former farm that now preserves pristine kettle bogs and will include a 165-acre manmade prairie.

Munroe Falls Metro Park nearly doubled in size with the 2007 addition of the Tallmadge Meadows Area, adjacent to the Summit County

A close-up of the floating mats that make up Young's Bogs at Springfield Bog Metro Park

In the summer of 2011, Indian blanket was one of the first plants to bloom in the manmade prairie at Springfield Bog.

Fairgrounds. It opened May 4, 2011 with two new hiking trails. A singular feature of the new area is the pauper's cemetery, a remnant of the former County Home, which naturalists will research and interpret during guided programs.

The Twinsburg Ledges Area at Liberty Park is planned to open in fall 2011 after much planning to preserve it. Opening the ledges without some limits could have damaged the fragile ecosystem, where moss covers the sandstone, cool air rises from the crevasses, endangered Indiana bats have been recorded and sensitive salamanders call the waters home.

The district's first park in Hudson, Wood Hollow Metro Park, is slated to be dedicated in 2012. It sits at the corner northwest corner of Barlow and Stow roads thanks to a seventy-four-acre tract of land donated anonymously in 2009 by a local family. The wooded area will have one hiking trail traveling through woods and some small wetlands.

A kingbird takes flight in the Tallmadge Meadows Area, the part of Munroe Falls Metro Park that opened in May 2011

Confluence Metro Park, south of Akron, will capitalize on the region's canal and water history when it opens in several years. Converging at the southern terminus of the Portage Path—used for centuries by Indians to portage canoes between the Cuyahoga and Tuscarawas rivers—the area includes parts of Barberton, Akron and Portage Lakes State Park. Eventually, trails through this area may connect with Firestone Metro Park and possibly the Ohio & Erie Canal Towpath Trail.

The park district is expanding its linear parks, or multi-purpose trails, with the completion of the last half-mile of the Towpath Trail, to be completed in late 2011, and the new 8.5-mile Freedom Secondary Trail,

When it opens, Wood Hollow will be the first Metro Park in Hudson. The planned hiking trail will traverse woods and wetlands.

another rails-to-trail project like the Bike & Hike Trail, which will connect Akron and Kent after its completion in several years.

Metro Parks is also following a rapidly growing interest in state-designated scenic water trails for use by human-powered canoes and kayaks. Sections of the Cuyahoga River and the Tuscarawas River watersheds, including the Ohio & Erie Canal and the Portage Lakes, are being analyzed for improvements and state designation.

Ninety years after its creation, there is still more space for Metro Parks, Serving Summit County to preserve. Its story continues.

Appendix

Mission

The mission of Metro Parks, Serving Summit County is to acquire, conserve and manage natural resources and to provide the public with safe, outdoor recreational and educational opportunities through a system of regional, natural-area parks.

Appointing Probate Judges

The Summit County Probate Judge appoints the three-member Board of Park Commissioners. The following judges have served in this capacity since the park district was established in 1921:

Lewis D. Slusser	1917–33
Dean F. May	1933–49
Vincent Zurz	1949–63
Nathan Koplin	1963–79
James V. Barbuto	1979–80
Nathan Koplin	1980
Willard F. Spicer	1980–2011

Board of Park Commissioners

The following individuals have served on the board during the park district's ninety-year history:

James Shaw,
1923–24

C.B. Raymond,
1923–25

Maude I. Milar,
1923–29

Edmund D.
Eckroad, 1925–33

F.A. Seiberling,
1925–34

Frank H. Adams,
1930–32

Mark M. Kindig,
1933–53

L.A. Laursen,
1934–41

Tracy A. Douglas,
1935–36

Mary M. Kinsey,
1936–46

Pearl L. Laursen,
1942

Henry G. Metzger,
1943–57

Walton A.
Woodling,
1947–63

Hezzleton E.
Simmons, 1954

Waldo L. Semon,
1955–69

Forrest D. Myers,
1958–73

Joseph W. Thomas,
1963–67

Edwin J. Thomas,
1968–76

M. Gerald O'Neil,
1969–78

Howard C. Walker,
1973

Richard W. Corns,
1973–76

John L. Tormey,
1976–85

Ronald D. Glosser,
1977–79

Robert E. Billman,
1978–87

Delores G.
Botnick, 1980–82

Charles J. Pilliod
Jr, 1983–86

William C. Zekan,
1985–90

Robert E. Mercer,
1986–94

William W.
Blodgett, 1987–90

David L. Brennan,
1990–95

John R. Ong,
1991–92

Thomas R.
Merryweather,
1992–93

Rainy G. Stitzlein,
1994–2009

Stanley C. Gault,
1995–96

Hoyt M. Wells,
1996–2003

Carol M. Curtis,
2003–present

Roland H. Bauer,
2010–present

Frances S.
Buchholzer,
1995–present

 Appendix

Director-Secretaries

Commissioners appoint the director-secretary, who serves as the chief executive officer and performs duties as board secretary.

Harold S. Wagner	1925–58
Forrest B. Coup	1958–63
Dr. Arthur T. Wilcox	1963–64
John R. Daily	1965–95
Thomas J. Shuster	1995–97
Keith D. Shy	1998–present

Park District Overview

As of January 2011, Metro Parks managed 10,500 acres, including 14 developed parks, 6 conservation areas and more than 125 miles of trails, with the 33.5-mile Bike & Hike Trail and 21.5 miles of the Ohio & Erie Canal Towpath Trail.

PARK	ACRES
Cascade Valley	543
Deep Lock Quarry	73
F.A. Seiberling Nature Realm	104
Firestone	258
Furnace Run	890
Goodyear Heights	410
Gorge	155
Hampton Hills	655
Liberty	1,759
Munroe Falls	509
O'Neil Woods	295
Sand Run	994
Silver Creek	624
Springfield Bog	256

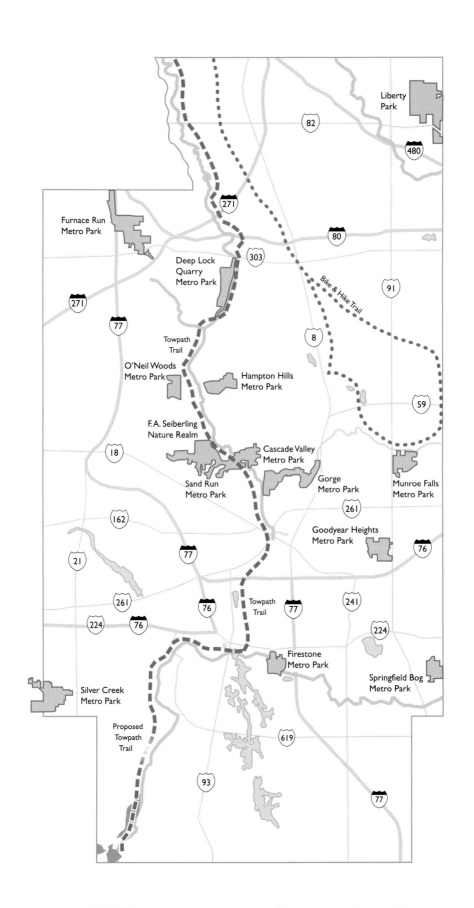

Sources

Chapter 1

Patricia M. Zonsius, *75 Years of Treasures and Pleasures: Metro Parks, Serving Summit County 1921–1996* (Akron, Ohio: Metro Parks, Serving Summit County, 1998), p. 7.

Harold S. Wagner, interview by J. Penfield Seiberling, May 1971, Metro Parks Administrative Offices, Akron, Ohio.

Oct. 5, 1925 report from the Olmsted Brothers, Park Correspondence, Metro Parks Collection, Akron-Summit County Public Library.

Chapter 2

Mabel Norris, ".2 Acre Started Big Park System," *Akron Beacon Journal*, Oct. 16, 1936, p. 25.

Wagner, interview by Seiberling.

Richfield Community News and Calendar, June 1977, p. 8.

Bert Szabo, "The Brushwood Boulder," *Woodland Trails*, June 1977.

Carl Dangel, *Akron Beacon Journal*, Aug. 26, 1959.

Charles Conaway, "Cuyahoga River Gorge could be a play spot," *Plain Dealer*, June 12, 1955, p. B8.

Akron Metropolitan Park District Board of Commissioners, Minutes, Nov. 17, 1936, Metro Parks Administrative Offices, Akron, Ohio.

Gilbert Waltz, short autobiography, p. 3, Metro Parks Collection, Akron-Summit County Public Library.

"New tract is added to East Akron park," *Akron Beacon Journal*, Feb. 11, 1930, p. 30.

"Proposal Submitted to The Board of Control of The Ohio Agricultural Experimental Station re: Virginia Kendall State Park by the Board of Park Commissioners of the Akron Metropolitan Park District," Aug. 13, 1932, Metro Parks Collection, Akron-Summit County Public Library.

Don Strouse, "Feudal Barony is Akron Play Spot," *Akron Beacon Journal*, Oct. 2, 1933.

Chapter 3

"New Park Levy Will Soon Bear initial Fruits," *Akron Times Press*, May 30, 1929.

Sand Run Water Supply Job justification, Dec. 16, 1940, Park Correspondence, Metro Parks Collection, Akron-Summit County Public Library.

"Six mile Bridle path is planned following gift," *Akron Beacon Journal*, July 6, 1930.

Park board files, Sand Run violations, Metro Parks Collection, Akron-Summit County Public Library.

Joe Jesensky, interview by author, Feb. 6, 2008.

Russell Happolt to H.S. Wagner, Oct. 2, 1930, Park Correspondence, Metro Parks Collection, Akron-Summit County Public Library.

Proposed nursery extension program for 1929, Park Correspondence, Metro Parks Collection, Akron-Summit County Public Library.

Letter to county health director RH Markwith, 1931, Park Correspondence, Metro Parks Collection, Akron-Summit County Public Library.

Akron Metropolitan Park District, Minutes, Feb. 25, 1933; Dec. 18, 1933; June 29, 1945, Metro Parks Administrative Offices, Akron, Ohio.

Park records, Sand Run, Metro Parks Collection, Akron-Summit County Public Library.

Ron Cockrell, "Recreation Comes to the Cuyahoga Valley: Activities of the Civilian Conservation Corps," in *A Green Shrouded Miracle: The Administrative History of the Cuyahoga Valley National Recreation Area* (Omaha, Neb.: National Park Service, 1992).

H.S. Wagner to U.S. Rep. Dow Harter, May 12, 1933, Park Correspondence, Metro Parks Collection, Akron-Summit County Public Library.

H.S. Wagner to U.S. Rep. Dow Harter, May 14, 1941, Park Correspondence, Metro Parks Collection, Akron-Summit County Public Library.

Chapter 4

"Anita Talks Father Into Busman's Holiday," *Akron Beacon Journal*, Oct. 8, 1964.

"When in Rome . . . So Aussies Went Hiking," *Akron Beacon Journal*, Dec. 2, 1965.

Chapter 5

Akron Metropolitan Park District Board of Commissioners, Minutes, June 15, 1929, Metro Parks Administrative Offices, Akron, Ohio.

Maude W. Milar to park commissioners, March 13, 1930, Park Correspondence, Metro Parks Collection, Akron-Summit County Public Library.

John Gammeter to Harold Wagner, 1930, Park Correspondence, Metro Parks Collection, Akron-Summit County Public Library.

Zonsius, *75 Years*, pp. 11–12.

Helen Coup, interview by Patricia M. Zonsius, 1997, Metro Parks Administrative Offices, Akron, Ohio.

Harold S. Wagner to Maude W. Milar, Aug. 25, 1929, Park Correspondence, Metro Parks Collection, Akron-Summit County Public Library.

Bert L. Szabo, interview by author, Feb. 5, 2007.

Chapter 6

Akron Metropolitan Park District Board of Commissioners, Minutes, Oct. 17, 1951, Metro Parks Administrative Offices, Akron, Ohio.

Kenneth Avery, interview by author, Jan. 12, 2009.

Cockrell, "Building Momentum to Preserve the Cuyahoga Valley," in *A Green Shrouded Miracle*.

Akron Metropolitan Park District Board of Commissioners, Minutes, June
    11, 1965; Oct. 8, 1971, Metro Parks Administrative Offices, Akron,
    Ohio.

Chapter 7

Walter Sheppe, Tour guide manual, May 1995, Cascade Locks Park
    Association, Metro Parks Collection, Akron-Summit County Public
    Library.
Zonsius, *75 Years*, p. 6.
Oct. 5, 1925 report from the Olmsted Brothers, pp. 12–13.
Tom Long, interview by author, Jan. 13, 2009.
Akron Metropolitan Park District Board of Commissioners, Minutes, April
    3, 1958; May, 17, 1972; Sept. 4, 1975; Sept. 25, 1979; Sept. 16,
    1981, Metro Parks Administrative Offices, Akron, Ohio.

Chapter 8

Jim Carney, "Ex-Girl Scouts reunite in forest," *Akron Beacon Journal*,
    Aug. 4, 2008.
Akron Metropolitan Park District Board of Commissioners, Minutes, Sept.
    9, 1958; Nov. 9, 1971, Metro Parks Administrative Offices, Akron,
    Ohio.
Minutes, Friends of the Metro Parks, Jan. 16, 1991, Metro Parks Admin-
    istrative Offices, Akron, Ohio.
Bob and Christine Freitag, interview by author, May 27, 2008.
www.akronzoo.org/about/history.asp.
Vivian Harig, interview by author, Feb. 16, 2009.
Board of Commissioners, Metro Parks, Serving Summit County, Minutes,
    Oct. 8, 1991, Nov. 20,1991, Metro Parks Administrative Offices,
    Akron, Ohio.